Promise Nation

Contents

Figures

Tables

Acknowledgments

I appreciate the support of the W.E. Upjohn Institute, including research assistance from Spencer Kennedy and Salwa Tareen, and comments provided by Timothy Bartik, Randy Eberts, Saleem Ghubril, Brad Hershbein, Lila Philips, Bridget Timmeney, and Chuck Wilbur. I also thank Richard Wyrwa, Allison Hewitt Colosky, and Erika Jackson for editorial and production support.

Chapter 1

What Is a Promise Scholarship Program?

Denver, Colorado—a booming city of 650,000 in the foothills of the Rocky Mountains; El Dorado, Arkansas—a company town of fewer than 20,000 located a few miles north of the Louisiana border; Kalamazoo, Michigan—a midsized city with a history of innovation in pharmaceuticals and medical technology; Pittsburgh, Pennsylvania—a city of 305,000 once known as "Steel City" and now rebounding from the loss of heavy industry. What do these four communities have in common? They are all leaders in a recent trend in college access that has spread rapidly across the United States. Place-based scholarships, often called "Promise" programs, have emerged in communities of all types and sizes, including those above, with about 50 in operation as of 2015. These four programs alone—the Kalamazoo Promise, Denver Scholarship Foundation, Pittsburgh Promise, and El Dorado Promise—have sent more than 15,000 students to college for free or close to it. The results are impressive.

- Following decades of decline, enrollment in the Kalamazoo Public Schools (KPS) grew 24 percent between 2005 and 2013. The availability of the Promise led to a reduction in suspensions, an increase in credits attempted, and, for African American students, a higher GPA. Recent data show a 33 percent increase in college completion among Kalamazoo students, with especially large benefits among minority and low-income students.[1]

- The college enrollment rate for graduates of Denver Public Schools rose from 37 percent to 51 percent between 2007 and 2012. The college persistence rate has increased to 79 percent, while for low-income, minority students the college retention rate reached 80 percent in 2013.[2]

- The high school graduation rate in the Pittsburgh Public Schools rose from 63 percent to 72 percent in the six years after the Pittsburgh Promise was introduced in 2008, and the college enrollment rate increased from 58 percent to 68 percent.[3]

- For graduates of the El Dorado School District, the college enrollment rate increased from 65 percent to over 90 percent between 2006 and 2013; 91 percent of freshmen completed their first year of college. Years of declining enrollment in the El Dorado School District have been reversed, and the district is now growing.[4]

At a time of intense national debate over the costs and benefits of college, local communities are finding ways to make higher education affordable and improve student outcomes. But the agenda for Promise stakeholders goes beyond college access and school improvement, as Promise programs also seek to transform the communities in which they are rooted.

The Promise model has been spreading quickly, but efforts to collectively analyze these programs are limited (see Andrews [2013]; LeGower and Walsh [2014]; and Miller-Adams [2009b, 2015]). There are reasons why this is a challenging task. These initiatives originate from the grassroots, are only loosely connected to each other, and differ in some of their fundamental features. Yet they represent an important departure from historical patterns of student financial aid and an innovative approach to community and economic development. This volume takes a broad look at the emergence and development of place-based scholarships and provides a nontechnical audience with some analytical tools for understanding both the origins and impact of Promise programs.

In this chapter, I define a Promise program, which is harder than it sounds since the current place-based scholarship programs differ from each other in many ways, both large and small. In Chapter 2, I address how Promise programs fit into the larger landscape of financial aid, economic development, and community change strategies, resolving some of the confusion that surrounds various "Promise"-named initiatives at the federal, state, and local levels. Chapter 3 explores the pathways through which the Promise model has expanded into new communities, a puzzling phenomenon given that the Promise movement lacks any central direction. Chapter 4 examines the two most critical design choices made by Promise stakeholders—which students are eligible for a scholarship and what institutions they can attend. While these decisions should relate to a community's critical need, all too often they do not, yet it is these structural choices that will determine the impact of a given Promise program. Chapter 5 reviews existing research and draws some conclusions about the impact of Promise programs to date. The research agenda is far from complete, but the state of knowledge is growing rapidly, making it possible to take stock of what we know thus far about what, in fact, Promise programs can be expected to accomplish. Chapter 6 looks at the area of impact that is hardest to measure or assess—how Promise programs affect economic development. Here, a number of issues make it difficult to assign causality, but there are very real ways in which place-based scholarships affect the local economy. Chapter 7 offers some concluding thoughts on the future of the Promise movement, its staying power, and the key issues to which Promise communities must attend. Here's a hint: It's not just about the money.

KALAMAZOO POINTS THE WAY

In November 2005, Kalamazoo, Michigan, became home to an unprecedented experiment in education-based economic renewal when Dr. Janice Brown, the then superintendent of KPS, announced that a group of anonymous donors had created the Kalamazoo Promise, a scholarship program that guarantees in perpetuity generous college scholarships to every student who graduates from the district, having met minimum enrollment and residency requirements. Behind the scholarship is an ambitious economic development agenda that seeks to revitalize the city and the region through a substantial investment in public education. The unorthodox approach drew widespread attention from national media and leaders in dozens of communities across the nation.[5]

The Kalamazoo Promise differs from most other scholarship programs in that the allocation of funds is based not on merit or need but on place.[6] Beginning with the class of 2006, every KPS graduate who has been enrolled in and resided in the district since kindergarten receives a scholarship covering 100 percent of tuition and mandatory fees at in-state, postsecondary institutions. Graduates who have attended a KPS school and lived in the district for four years receive a scholarship covering 65 percent of these costs, with a sliding scale for those in between. Scholarships are awarded on a first-dollar basis, meaning that the scholarship amount is calculated before a student's other grant aid. Students eligible for additional aid, usually in the form of federal Pell Grants, can use their non-Promise aid to pay for room and board or other college costs. (Most students in KPS, with a low-income enrollment rate of about 70 percent, will be eligible for federal financial aid.) For the graduating classes of 2006 to 2014, the scholarship could be used at any one of Michigan's 43 public colleges or universities. For the class of 2015 and beyond, 15 private liberal arts colleges, all members of the Michigan Colleges Alliance, are included as postsecondary options. Recipients have 10 years after high school graduation in which to use their scholarship funding. There are almost no strings attached: students must maintain a 2.0 GPA in their college courses and make regular progress toward a degree in order to continue receiving the scholarship.

The results of the program have included surprises, some of which are positive for the local economy—almost two-thirds of scholarship recipients have chosen to attend a local postsecondary institution, and there has been a dramatic increase in college completion—others less so—it has been difficult to detect any positive impact for the local housing market. But there is no bigger surprise than what has happened outside Kalamazoo. Spurred in part by extensive national media coverage and the reporting (and misreporting) of early positive results from the Kalamazoo Promise, communities in every part of the country have created their own place-based scholarship programs inspired by what is happening in Kalamazoo.

The first cities to announce their intentions to develop Promise-type programs did so only a few months after the introduction of the Kalamazoo Promise. These included Newton, Iowa, a company town adjusting to the imminent departure of the Maytag Corporation; Hammond, Indiana, a shrinking industrial city on the southern shore of Lake Michigan; and Flint, Michigan, the distressed former home to General Motors' main production facilities and the setting for Michael Moore's classic anticorporate documentary, *Roger and Me*. By the first anniversary of the Kalamazoo Promise announcement in November 2006, the floodgates had opened, with city after city announcing its own version of the program. Some of these plans have come to fruition, while others have not.[7]

Three of the programs mentioned above—the Denver Scholarship Foundation, the El Dorado Promise, and the Pittsburgh Promise —were created in the 2006–2007 period and represent some of the earliest Promise programs. They also underscore the difficulty of generalizing about this group of initiatives.

Although these programs were inspired by the Kalamazoo Promise, only one mirrors the fundamental premise of the Kalamazoo program: that all students should be eligible for a scholarship, receiving funding to attend any postsecondary institution to which they can gain admission. (Even very short-term career and technical programs offered by community colleges, as well as one apprenticeship program and a vocational training school for special needs students, are covered by the Kalamazoo Promise.) The El Dorado Promise adopted this universal approach as well as the first-dollar structure, providing even greater flexibility than the Kalamazoo Promise by allowing students to use their scholarships at any accredited two- or four-year, public or private educational institution in the United States. (Tuition is capped at the highest annual resident tuition at an Arkansas public university.) In 2013, the El Dorado Promise further broadened student eligibility by removing the residency requirement, meaning that any student attending El Dorado Public Schools, regardless of whether he or she resides within the school district, is eligible for the scholarship.

The Denver and Pittsburgh programs both departed from the universal eligibility approach of the Kalamazoo and El Dorado scholarships, but they did so in different ways. Denver's is one of a handful of Promise scholarship programs that has a financial need component—in order to qualify, family income must fall within one-and-a-half times the Pell Grant limit (here, too, the school district's free and reduced-price lunch rate of over 70 percent means that a majority of students are indeed eligible). The program also funds undocumented students with lawful presence who are not eligible for federal aid. It requires a 2.0 high school GPA, or a C average, for receipt of a scholarship. The maximum amount of scholarship funding available is lower than that offered by the El Dorado or Kalamazoo programs; however, recipients are required to apply for at least three other scholarships in addition to completing the Free Application for Federal Student Aid (FAFSA), which means that substantial additional grant aid has been leveraged.

A large part of the Denver Scholarship Foundation budget goes to support Future Centers serving 21 of the district's high schools. These centers are one-stop shops for college awareness, financial aid, and the college application process, helping students access scholarship funding beyond that provided by the foundation itself.

The Pittsburgh Promise does not consider financial need, but it has stricter merit requirements than Denver's program, with eligibility for the scholarship contingent on a 2.5 GPA and 90 percent attendance rate in high school to qualify for full funding of up to $7,500 a year for four years.[8] (As with most Promise programs, the amount of the scholarship is prorated for the number of years a student has attended the school district.) There is a provision for students with

GPAs in the 2.0–2.5 range to receive support to attend the local community college and transition to full eligibility if they are successful in that environment. This merit-based model has been adopted by many other communities with some variations; the New Haven Promise, for example, requires a 3.0 GPA.

As of this writing, about half of the existing Promise programs have a merit component to eligibility, while half have opted for universal eligibility, as in Kalamazoo. Most Promise programs differ from Kalamazoo and El Dorado in another important respect: they are "last-dollar" programs, meaning that the Promise scholarship is awarded after other grant aid is calculated.

Many of the other communities that have launched Promise programs, including some that were announced in the very earliest days following the Kalamazoo Promise, limit use of the scholarship to local institutions. The Bay Commitment in Michigan, Ventura College Promise in California, and Garrett County Scholarship Program in Maryland are all examples of programs where students receive funding that can be used only at a local two-year institution.

Figure 1.1 shows the distribution of place-based scholarship programs as of 2015. This landscape is continually evolving, as new communities discover, plan, and implement Promise programs.[9] (Appendix A includes details about selected programs, while the W.E. Upjohn Institute website provides a more detailed and continually updated database.)

Given the diversity of their structure, does it make sense to treat Promise programs as a group? I would argue that it does, for two reasons. First, these programs all embody a place-based approach to awarding scholarships. Financial aid in the United States is generally awarded on the basis of need or academic merit. Such scholarships go to the individual student without regard to which school he or she attends. Beginning with the Kalamazoo Promise in 2005, and continuing well into the future (many more Promise programs are in the works), dozens of communities have opted to create scholarship programs where the key determinant of eligibility is long-

Figure 1.1 Distribution of Place-Based Scholarship Programs, 2015

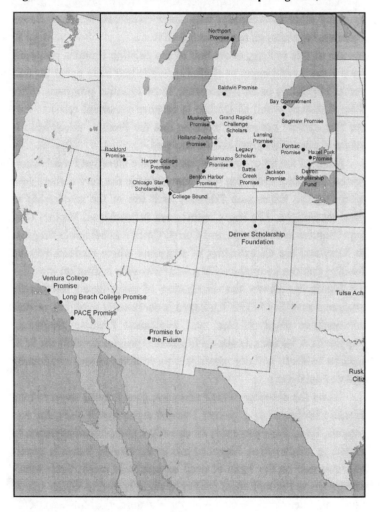

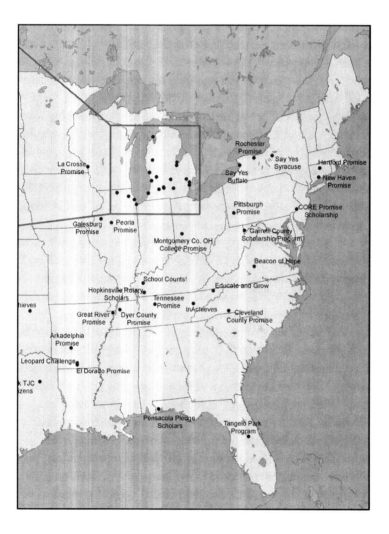

term attendance (and often residency) in a specific school district. This place-based model has existed in other forms, at a larger scale in statewide merit programs such as Georgia Hope, and at a smaller scale in scholarships extended to students at a single school or even a single grade within a school, such as the Tangelo Park and "I Have a Dream" programs.[10] The notion of awarding scholarships based on school district attendance and residency is a new idea and one that has taken hold in communities of many different types and sizes. There is an early-awareness component as well, with students knowing when they start school in a given school district that they will be eligible for the scholarship years down the road. Finally, these programs are explicitly very long term—the Kalamazoo Promise has been set up to continue in perpetuity, whereas other programs aim to create sustainable endowments or guarantee that their scholarships will continue for several decades. The long-term sustainability of funding is critical to the success of such programs. Whether communities can build a sustainable funding model is a critical question; some statewide merit programs (including Michigan's) have been eliminated because of state legislative action and economic conditions, raising skepticism about the viability of an ironclad, long-term guarantee.[11]

The second reason Promise programs can and should be analyzed as a group has to do with their goals. In surveying the stated motivations for establishing place-based scholarship programs, three themes emerge. The most obvious goal of Promise programs, as well as most other scholarship initiatives, is to *increase access to postsecondary education*. Promise programs do this by reducing the financial barrier to higher education through the provision of grant funding rather than loans. They also further this goal by providing support services, such as Future Centers or other college awareness and readiness programs, to help students overcome the nonfinancial barriers to postsecondary education. A second stated goal of most Promise programs is to *build a college-going culture* in the school district and surrounding community. This involves the types of access and awareness programs mentioned above, as well as an increase in college preparedness activities through, for example, early literacy initiatives, career awareness programs, expansion of advanced placement courses, and college visits. But it is the third category of goals that truly sets Promise programs apart from other scholarship initiatives and suggests that they should be viewed as a group: their emphasis on *local community and economic development*. Promise stakeholders have made it clear that these initiatives are not just about students and schools; they are also about transforming the communities in which these schools are located. In Chapter 6, I address the question of whether this is a realistic goal and what it means to say that a scholarship program can serve as a tool to promote community and economic development. For now, it is sufficient to note that most Promise stakeholders see their programs as tools to advance this larger agenda.

With these factors in mind, it is possible to arrive at a working definition, one that allows for the variations among these initiatives while acknowledging their common features: Promise programs seek to transform their communities by making a long-term investment in education through place-based scholarships. They all seek to expand access to and ensure success in higher education, deepen the college-going culture in both the K–12 system and community as a whole, and support local economic development.[12]

With a definition in hand, we can turn our attention to how such programs fit into the national landscape of college access, financial aid, and community transformation, the topics of Chapter 2.

Notes

1. For enrollment data, see Hershbein (2013). For achievement data, see Bartik and Lachowska (2012). For postsecondary outcomes data, see Bartik, Hershbein, and Lachowska (2015).
2. For details, see Pell Institute (2015) and the Denver Scholarship Foundation annual report: http://www.denverscholarship.org/sites/default/files/multi_file/subsection/download/DSF-13-14-AnnualReport-singlePage.pdf (accessed July 14, 2015).
3. See the Impact Dashboard of the Pittsburgh Promise: http://pittsburgh promise.org/about_dashboard.php (accessed July 14, 2015).

4. For more information, see the El Dorado Promise website: http://www.eldoradopromise.com and Ash and Ritter (2014).
5. For the full story of the introduction of the Kalamazoo Promise, see Miller-Adams (2009a).
6. For details, see the Kalamazoo Promise website: http://www.kalamazoopromise.com.
7. The Newton and Flint programs never got off the ground, although the College Bound program in Hammond continues to award scholarships to the children of homeowners in that community.
8. In July 2015, the Pittsburgh Promise reduced the level of the benefit it provides, lowering the annual maximum grant amount from $10,000 a year, or a maximum of $40,000, to $7,500 a year, or a maximum of $30,000. Equally important was a change in the costs covered, from the full cost of college to tuition and fees only. These changes were deemed necessary to be able to sustain the program's funding for the long term (see "Pittsburgh Promise Adjusts Program to Benefit More Pittsburgh Students" [2015]).
9. For example, as this book was going to press, basketball superstar LeBron James announced a scholarship for low-income students in partnership with the University of Akron that could benefit up to 2,300 Akron public school graduates (Schleis 2015).
10. The "I Have a Dream" model originated in 1981 when Dr. Eugene Lang promised to send every sixth grader at East Harlem's P.S. 121, the school he had attended 50 years earlier, to college for free provided they stayed in school through high-school graduation. The active "I Have a Dream" network currently comprises 16 affiliates operating 38 programs across the United States. See http://www.ihaveadreamfoundation.org for more information. Tangelo Park is a subdivision of Orlando, FL, where the Rosen Foundation Scholarship gives last-dollar support to any student going to college who resided in the subdivision for at least two years prior to graduation. The program dates from 1993.
11. In Kalamazoo, this is not a concern. On August 15, 2015, at a celebration of the tenth anniversary of the Kalamazoo Promise, Dr. Janice Brown read the first public statement made by the anonymous donors. In it, they pledged the following: "As donors, we are humbled and proud to commit that we will be with you for generations to come" (Mack 2015a).
12. Andrews (2013) defines a Promise program "as a local place-based scholarship program that offers near-universal access to funding for postsecondary education. Information about this funding reaches potential recipients well in advance of the decision to acquire post-secondary education" (p. 2).

Chapter 2

The National Landscape

*P*_{romise} is a powerful word. Both a noun and a verb, it is loaded with multiple meanings. It can be used as an assurance that something will happen or signify an expectation that an outcome (usually good) will materialize. It is no surprise, then, that the word has often been used in conjunction with college scholarship programs, which constitute both a commitment to supporting students and the notion that doing so will yield some kind of positive return. Several statewide merit aid programs have opted to call themselves Promise programs—Oklahoma's Promise dates from the early 1990s, the state of Washington's from 1999, and West Virginia's from 2002. In 2006, Michigan renamed its merit aid program the "Michigan Promise" scholarship; of course, promises can be broken, and this one fell victim to legislative funding cuts in 2009.

The federal government, too, has gotten into the Promise game. In 2010, the Obama administration introduced its Promise Neighborhoods initiative through which $100 million was directed to 58 communities "to significantly improve the educational and developmental outcomes of children and youth in our most distressed communities."[1] The Promise Neighborhoods program, proposed during the 2008 campaign by then candidate Obama, is modeled on the cradle-to-career approach of the Harlem Children's Zone. Congress failed to re-fund the program in 2013, but while no new programs are receiving grants, many communities had already launched cradle-to-career initiatives partly in response to the federal government's three-year funding program. As the Promise Neighborhoods program wound down, in 2013 the Obama administration announced Promise Zones, a new initiative in which the federal government will partner with local communities and businesses to create jobs, increase economic security, expand educational opportunities, increase access to quality, affordable housing, and improve public safety. The first five Promise

13

Zones were named in January 2014, with another eight announced in April of the following year. A third round of applications for Promise Zone funding began in the summer of 2015. Promise Zones do not receive funding but benefit from technical assistance and preferential access to existing federal funding streams (U.S. Department of Housing and Urban Development n.d.).

The state of Michigan already had its own Promise Zones—scholarship programs in 10 low-income communities inspired by the Kalamazoo Promise and funded through private donations, need-based aid, and future growth in the State Education Tax. Proposed in 2007 by the then governor Jennifer Granholm and signed into law in 2009, 8 of these zones were granting scholarships by 2013, although funding levels are lower and postsecondary options generally more limited than in Kalamazoo. In 2014, the Tennessee Promise, proposed by Governor Bill Haslam, became the most expansive Promise program to date, covering tuition and fees (after federal aid is calculated) at community colleges for every student in the state beginning with the class of 2015. This is the first time since the mid-twentieth century (when public education systems in California were largely free) that a state has made community college free to all its residents. Oregon passed similar legislation in 2015 (although, unlike Tennessee, it includes a merit provision), and other states are likely to follow. In his 2015 State of the Union address, President Obama cited the Tennessee Promise as a precedent for his America's College Promise proposal that would make community college free through a federal–state partnership (White House 2015).

It is not always clear whether or how these various Promise-named initiatives have influenced each other. The Promise scholarship movement that is the focus of this book emerged from within local communities and is now inspiring a new generation of state-level programs, while federal Promise programs were developed independently of these grassroots efforts. Yet in a broader sense, these initiatives are part of the same family of place-based initiatives that seek to transform their communities through a focus on education. They also require deep community alignment, often organized within a collective impact framework, to accomplish this transformative goal.

To explore the connections among these various Promise threads, this chapter examines Promise scholarship programs in relation to the broader issues of student financial aid, place-based economic development, and collective impact approaches to social change.

PROMISE PROGRAMS AS FINANCIAL AID

The recognition of the need for some kind of postsecondary education and training has been growing in the United States over the past three decades as globalization and technological change have squeezed low-skilled workers and put a premium on a college education. In the years since the Kalamazoo Promise was announced, the "college for all" movement has intensified, especially as the fallout from the 2008 recession underscored the value of a college degree in terms of both protection against unemployment and earning power (see Figure 2.1 and Hershbein and Hollenbeck [2015]).

During the Obama administration's second term, efforts to rein in student loan debt and promote college access and completion took off, with pressure from the White House placed on colleges and universities to ensure that students graduate on time and new national efforts, including a College Scorecard, to provide students with information about the real cost of a college education.[2] At the state level, the development of statewide and local college access networks provided additional momentum by educating students about how to prepare for and apply to college, search for scholarships, and obtain financial aid. The academic community weighed in with demonstration projects showing the value of automatic FAFSA completion (Bettinger, Long, and Oreopoulous 2013), proposing ways to simplify the FAFSA (Dynarski and Scott-Clayton 2007), and providing information to high-achieving, low-income students to reduce undermatching (Hoxby and Turner 2013).[3]

**Figure 2.1   Earnings and Unemployment Rates by
Educational Attainment**

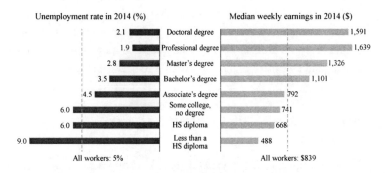

NOTE: Data are for persons age 25 and over. Earnings are for full-time wage and salary workers.
SOURCE: Current Population Survey, U.S. Bureau of Labor Statistics, U.S. Department of Labor.

Throughout this period, college costs continued to rise, with tuition increases outpacing inflation at every type of institution as state legislatures cut back on higher education funding, and the recession put added pressure on endowments and state finances. Rising student loan debt and poor college completion rates, especially at two-year and for-profit institutions, have generated some pushback to the "college for all" movement. Part of the problem with this debate is how the term *college* is used. If defined broadly to include career and technical training, it is arguable that some kind of postsecondary education and training is indeed required for most everyone, as wages for those with a high school diploma (or less) are at a 50-year low and job opportunities very limited—precisely the argument made by the president in his 2015 State of the Union address. All too often, however, people refer to the term college as a four-year, degree-granting institution, and many students set off down that path without adequate preparedness or motivation, leading to poor completion rates and a college experience that is of limited value in the workplace. State college access networks have led the way in promoting the use of the term college in its broadest sense or replacing it with the phrase "postsecondary education and training."

Often overlooked in this state and national landscape are localized efforts by individual communities to dramatically lower not only the cost of higher education but also the informational and cultural barriers to accessing financial aid that deter many first-generation college-goers from pursuing postsecondary education.

Most fundamentally, Promise scholarship programs break from the traditional approach to financial aid, which is awarded based on some measure of financial need or academic merit, by granting scholarships based on place. In most Promise programs, the level of scholarship funding is related to the length of a student's enrollment in a given K–12 school district and usually his or her residency within that district's boundaries. State merit aid programs are analogous in that they too are residency based and are motivated in part by the economic development goal of retaining high-achieving students instate for their college years and hopefully beyond. But state merit programs are at a much larger scale, are considerably less generous, and all include merit requirements in the form of minimum GPAs (Dynarski 2004).

The Kalamazoo Promise technically was not the first place-based scholarship program at the level of a single school district—that distinction goes to the small town of Philomath, Oregon, which benefited from a similar program beginning in 1959 (for details, see Miller-Adams [2009a, pp. 59–61])—but it is the first on a large scale and the first of the current era. Moreover, the Kalamazoo Promise is unique in its scope and simplicity, being structured as a first-dollar program, giving students 10 years after high school graduation in which to use their scholarship funding, and continuing in perpetuity. These generous features, along with the mystery of the anonymous donors, attracted national attention and sparked a process of replication that has led to the adoption of the place-based model in dozens of communities.

Only one other program to date—the El Dorado Promise—awards its funding on a first-dollar basis, but other elements of the Kalamazoo Promise have been widely emulated. All Promise programs embrace the place-based concept, a few have added a family income ceiling, and many have added some kind of merit requirement, usually a minimum GPA. These merit-based programs are qualitatively different from the Kalamazoo Promise and other universal eligibility programs, essentially mirroring statewide merit-based programs for a smaller geographic unit. The structure of Promise scholarship programs requires a different mode of analysis than that of traditional financial aid. Because they reach so many students within a single school building, Promise programs have schoolwide effects that scholarships awarded to select students in their senior year do not. These schoolwide effects, especially the impact of peers, must be accounted for in any study of impact. Similarly, while traditional scholarships affect individual students, Promise programs create incentives for school districts themselves to innovate. The resulting changes in school climate, teacher and parent expectations, and the role of community members in providing support to students must also be addressed by education researchers. Promise scholarships are likely to attract new students into a district; if these students are qualitatively different from the students attending when the program was announced, researchers must control for changes in the composition of the student body. Finally, Promise scholarships have explicit economic development goals, seeking to retain and attract families within school district or city boundaries; hence, research attention must be directed outside the educational system to identify and track these community-level impacts, which might include migration, business development, or housing market improvements.

PROMISE PROGRAMS AS ECONOMIC DEVELOPMENT

As noted above, Promise programs are about more than scholarships for students. They are also about transforming the communities in which students reside. Although the Kalamazoo Promise donors have opted to remain anonymous, they have made clear through surrogates that the economic revitalization of their city is one of the goals of the scholarship program they created. Subsequent Promise programs, regardless of eligibility criteria, embrace economic development goals as part of their agenda.

The clearest indication of an economic development agenda behind the Kalamazoo Promise and many other such programs is its residency requirement. In order to benefit from the Kalamazoo Promise, a student must not only attend KPS for a minimum of four years but also reside within the district's boundaries. This is widely interpreted as a strategy to draw families into the area's urban core and retain those already residing there.

Most other Promise programs have similar residency requirements, with the largest scholarship amounts going to the longest-term residents. In 2013, the El Dorado Promise changed this rule, allowing students who reside outside the district but attend school there to receive the scholarship. In essence, this represents a reasonable bet that a growing public school district will benefit a city, even if some students live outside that city's boundaries.

Beyond simply attracting new residents and families to places that are usually declining in population, Promise programs represent one avenue toward creating a better-educated workforce in the local community. The path through which this is likely to occur, however, is often misunderstood. Some people invest in Promise programs believing that, down the road, the better-educated graduates of a given school district will remain in or return to the community, increasing the educational level of its workforce. It should be recognized that although some local residents will remain in (or return to) their home area—perhaps 40–50 percent—many will not. Furthermore, any local economic development plan that relies on the higher skills of today's children will necessarily be very long term—it takes an entire generation and more to transform the skills of the workforce simply through educating a community's children. However, more immediate economic development impacts, often on a large scale, can be achieved by attracting parents today, and thereby attracting employers in the next few years. Efforts to strengthen the quality of a school district, particularly one that serves low-income students, will benefit a community's economy by making that district and community more attractive to educated workers who might consider moving to it, as well as to employers who are seeking educated workers (more on this in Chapter 6).

Place-based economic development is nothing new. For half a century, cities, regions, and states have pursued localized strategies to attract business and residents, expand the tax base, and increase jobs for residents. These efforts have included investments in infrastructure, the provision of tax incentives for business to relocate or expand locally, and quality of life improvements that make a community more desirable to mobile workers. (The Obama administration's Promise Zones is the latest iteration of federal support for such initiatives.) Increasingly, though, there is an emphasis on investing in human capital development to give communities a critical edge in attracting employers and educated residents. The Promise movement takes this human capital orientation to a new level with an economic development strategy based on the provision of college scholarships to a large segment of a community's young people.

PROMISE PROGRAMS AND COLLECTIVE IMPACT STRATEGIES

Promise programs bear a resemblance to cradle-to-career initiatives, which seek to align community resources in support of improved outcomes for vulnerable youth. The model for many of these is the Harlem Children's Zone, a multifaceted set of interventions that began in the 1990s and grew into an integrated web of services supporting youth in a 97-block area in central Harlem. Communities around the country have emulated the Harlem Children's Zone by selecting a geographically bounded area and building a cradle-to-career pipeline of support that focuses on critical points of intervention along the developmental continuum. These types of initiatives seek to overcome the shortcomings of traditional antipoverty policy by breaking down silos between overlapping and uncoordinated programs, increasing impact through tighter alignment of multiple partners, and promoting accountability through the use of data systems to track impact and improve design.

Many of these strategies take place within what has come to be called a collective impact framework. *Collective impact* is a term used to describe multisector efforts to enact large-scale social change. While such efforts have a long history, this terminology is relatively new; in fact, collective impact was chosen as the number-two philanthropy buzzword for 2011 (Bernholz 2011). FSG, one of the leading consultants in the field, explains that "collective impact occurs when organizations from different sectors agree to solve a specific social problem using a common agenda, aligning their efforts, and using common measures of success" (FSG n.d., p. 22). Writing in the *Stanford Social Innovation Review* about Strive, another leading consulting organization in the field, Kania and Kramer (2011) define collective impact as "a structured process that leads to a common agenda, shared measurement, continuous communication, and mutually reinforcing activities among all participants" (p. 38). Ideally, collective impact efforts will involve everyone in a community—government and educational institutions (K–12 and postsecondary); local businesses, including philanthropies and nonprofits; individual students; teachers; parents; interested citizens; and organizational leaders.

While Promise scholarship programs emerged independently of this trend in social innovation, they have often served as catalysts for collective impact strategies in their respective communities. It is easy to understand why. Promise scholarship programs seek broad goals—increase access to higher education, change the culture of the K–12 system, and promote local economic development—but they do so through a blunt tool at one point late on the developmental continuum, the provision of college scholarships. In Promise communities, it has rapidly become clear that reducing the cost of higher education is only the first step toward achieving these broad goals. The process has played out in similar ways in multiple communities—the creation of place-based scholarship programs immediately highlights the need for better academic and social preparedness for high school graduates, which in turn raises the issue of achievement gaps throughout the K–12 system. These gaps direct community attention to disparities even earlier along the developmental continuum around the availability of high-quality preschool and kindergarten readiness. On the upper end of the continuum, Promise programs underscore the need for support at the postsecondary level to ensure that scholarship recipients don't just go to college but actually persist, progress, and complete some kind of certificate or degree that will be of value in the workforce. Almost before they know it, Promise stakeholders are faced with the need to attend to all the stages of the developmental continuum—indeed, from cradle (or even precradle) to career—in order for their scholarship programs to be a success.

Kalamazoo provides an excellent example of this dynamic. When the Kalamazoo Promise was announced, community members were thrilled by the prospect of an essentially unlimited pool of funds to send young people to college. But attention quickly shifted to the steps that would be needed to ensure the success of future scholarship beneficiaries. Community alignment efforts began almost immediately to address some of the challenges facing young people in this high-poverty community from birth on. One outcome was KC Ready 4s, a countywide strategy to provide universal, high-quality preschool to every child. The motivation was to boost achievement at an early stage in a significant but relatively low-cost way. At the other end of the continuum, community members worked to create a countywide college access network and align the services that support low-literacy adults. The Learning Network of Greater Kalamazoo, a collective impact strategy spearheaded by the local community foundation and funded in part by the W.K. Kellogg Foundation, was introduced in 2011 and is now affiliated with the StriveTogether Cradle to Career Network. While the Learning Network has struggled to gain traction in the broader community, it has increased public awareness of the benefits of collaboration and the alignment of resources around student success.

There is real uncertainty about whether a place-based scholarship can have a major effect on a community in the absence of the deep alignment characteristic of the best collective impact efforts. It is arguable that the most important function of a Promise scholarship program is in fact to serve as a catalyst for a more integrated web of support that serves young people from birth through the K–12 system, then through college and into the workforce. In some places, these support mechanisms are built into the scholarship program, such as the Denver Scholarship Foundation's Future Centers, the "Say Yes" model in Buffalo and Syracuse that couples scholarships with comprehensive in-school supports, and the wraparound services offered by early commitment programs such as Grand Rapids's Challenge Scholars. In other places, alignment efforts have been more diffuse and sometimes difficult to organize. But early research suggests that community alignment, whether organized formally through a collective impact strategy or more ad hoc, is in fact the critical element in whether Promise programs will ultimately achieve their goals, especially those related to transforming schools and communities.

Before turning to the impact of Promise programs, in the next chapter I examine the mechanisms through which this model spread and ask what it is about place-based scholarships that stakeholders in so many communities have found so compelling.

Notes

1. See the U.S. Department of Education Promise Neighborhoods website: http://www2.ed.gov/programs/promiseneighborhoods/index.html (accessed August 13, 2015).
2. See https://www.whitehouse.gov/issues/education/higher-education/college-score-card (accessed August 13, 2015).
3. Undermatching refers to the tendency of poor students to apply to schools for which they are overqualified rather than more selective schools that might provide them with a more valuable degree at a lower cost.

Chapter 3

The Diffusion of the Promise Idea

One of the most remarkable features of the Promise movement is that it has emerged without any central direction or leadership. Indeed, this is the great surprise of the Kalamazoo Promise: people in communities large and small, urban and rural, saw something in the model that made sense to them and then acted independently to adapt it to their local context. The result is an array of programs that share two fundamental features—the awarding of scholarships based on place and the goal of transforming both schools and communities—but that differ in many respects. On the one hand, variations in program design make it challenging to generalize about Promise scholarships, and on the other hand, they make possible comparisons that, if analyzed carefully, can yield findings about what works best.

In this chapter I explore why and how the place-based scholarship model introduced in Kalamazoo in 2005 has inspired people in other places to embark on similar experiments. It is a complex story, especially when compared to some of the initiatives mentioned in the previous chapter. The Promise Neighborhoods program, for example, gained national traction through a federal grant-making process. While only a few dozen grants were awarded, hundreds of communities applied for the program, going through the convening, alignment, and data collection steps necessary to produce a viable application. The collective impact idea has diffused through the activities of consulting firms such as FSG and Strive that work with communities to create local structures that mirror their model. As of mid-2015, the StriveTogether Cradle to Career Network included 63 partnerships in 32 states, meaning that these communities had adopted the core principles of collective impact according to Strive. Many more communities incorporate elements of Strive's approach without being part of the formal network. The rapid proliferation of place-based scholarship programs is harder to explain, as they emerged within a relatively short time frame without any central direction or technical assistance. Why has the Kalamazoo Promise generated such strong interest in replication? How did the model spread, and how has it been altered along the way to accommodate the needs of different communities? What mechanisms are in place to facilitate communication and information sharing among existing programs and invite new communities into the process? This chapter answers these questions.

PLACE-BASED SCHOLARSHIPS AND POLICY DIFFUSION

Political scientists attuned to issues of federalism have long studied how public policies emerge and spread across multiple communities. Much of this research focuses on how cities and states serve as policy laboratories for new ideas, how these ideas move from community to community, and how they sometimes bubble up from localities to states (Shipan and Volden 2012). All these mechanisms are at work in the diffusion of Promise scholarship programs. The place-based scholarship model is a local innovation that moved rapidly into multiple communities and has recently been adopted at the state level with the announcement of the Tennessee and Oregon Promise programs.

Shipan and Volden (2008) identify four separate mechanisms of policy diffusion: 1) learning, 2) competition, 3) imitation/emulation, and 4) coercion. The primary dynamic behind the diffusion of Promise programs to date is emulation. While stakeholders may believe they are learning from the experience of Kalamazoo and other early adopting communities, they are only partially correct, for a number of reasons. First, it is still too early to have definitive data on the impact of even the oldest Promise programs, although a more coordinated research and evaluation effort is emerging (see p. 40 and Chapter 7). Second, results from Kalamazoo have sometimes been misreported or misinterpreted, taking on a life of their own through media coverage. The best example is an early report that the introduction of the

Kalamazoo Promise had led to an increase in housing prices; while this has not been substantiated and, to date, there is no discernible impact of the Promise on housing prices, it was reported widely and used to garner support for Promise programs in many other communities. Third, the structure of Promise programs varies across communities, meaning that results in one place may have little relevance for another. The danger of "learning" under these conditions is that expectations are created that may not be met, which in turn can diminish public support and buy-in for what must be understood as a very long-term investment.

These problems are exacerbated by a lack of formal coordination or common evaluation framework among Promise programs, bringing us back to the question of how an idea championed by a handful of wealthy individuals in a small city in southwest Michigan took hold across the nation.

Through five editions of his book, *Diffusion of Innovations*, Everett M. Rogers (2003, p. 5) includes the following elements in his definition of policy diffusion:

An innovation is an idea, practice, or other object that is perceived as new by an individual or other unit of adoption. In this case, the innovation is a scholarship program based not on the individual attributes of recipients but on location, suggesting a local economic development rationale. Apart from some small-scale efforts, including the Philomath program, the Kalamazoo Promise was the first such example of this kind of scholarship program, and certainly the first to be widely publicized in the national media.

A communication system that facilitates the transmission of the new idea from one individual or group to another. Rogers identifies two critical communication channels: mass media ("usually the most rapid and efficient means of informing an audience of potential adopters about the existence of an innovation" [p. 18]) and interpersonal channels. He also mentions interactive communication via the Internet as a more recent but increasingly important phenomenon. In this case, national media played a critical role in transmitting awareness of the Promise model beyond the local community. Especially important were several *Associated Press* articles written shortly after the Kalamazoo Promise was introduced and picked up by newspapers around the nation, and subsequent coverage by major national news outlets that reach decision makers all over. Television played a role as well, with segments about the Kalamazoo Promise on the *Today Show*, *Good Morning America*, and the *CBS Evening News*. Once word was out, interpersonal communications channels took over, with a stream of individuals e-mailing, calling, and visiting Kalamazoo. The relationships formed through this process gave rise to the first PromiseNet conference in 2008 (see p. 38).

A social system that provides the domain for the diffusion process. The Promise model brings together different policy arenas, meaning that the diffusion process has played out in several different social systems. One of these is the community of educators and education policy researchers interested in school reform, college access, and financial aid. Another social system is that of economic development practitioners, where attention to the Kalamazoo Promise has been fostered through a series of awards and recognition of the model as an innovative approach to economic development. A third is the growing group of individuals interested in using collective impact strategies to enact large-scale social change.

Time for the innovation to spread from awareness to adoption throughout the social system. The rapidity with which the Promise model spread, with a dozen programs introduced in the two years after the Kalamazoo Promise was announced, suggests that it was emulation rather than learning at work in the diffusion process. In short, communities embarked on designing their own place-based scholarship programs because it sounded like a good idea, not on the basis of any tangible results. It is arguable that even today, a decade after the announcement of the Kalamazoo Promise, ongoing efforts to replicate it are more a matter of instinct or faith than of evidence-based decision making. (The body of evidence emerging around the impact of Promise programs is summarized in Chapter 5.)

Rogers's (2003) framework provides some insight into the factors that underpin the speed and breadth of a policy innovation. Among these are characteristics of the innovation itself, including its degree of complexity. One of the hallmarks of the Kalamazoo Promise is simplicity. The terms of the program fit easily on a palm card; the application form for the scholarship is one page long; and for its first three years a single administrator managed the entire tracking, application, approval, and disbursement process for all eligible students and postsecondary institutions. Rogers writes that "many adopters want to participate actively in customizing an innovation to fit their unique situation" (p. 17), arguing that an innovation diffuses more rapidly and its adoption is more likely to be sustained when it is subject to reinvention. It appears that the simplicity of the Kalamazoo Promise and the adaptability of its key features to a community's specific needs—in other words, the potential for reinvention—has been a powerful factor in the rapid diffusion of the model. But it is not just the structure of the place-based scholarship model that is responsible for its diffusion—the concept itself has proven deeply attractive.

THE PROMISE IDEA

Why is the place-based scholarship idea so compelling? The short answer is that it offers a simple and flexible tool to make communities more attractive to residents and businesses. A glance at the map of Promise programs in Chapter 1 (Figure 1, pp. 8–9) shows a strong cluster of Promise programs in the upper Midwest and Northeast. Some of this is due to the demonstration effect of the Kalamazoo Promise, which inspired the Michigan Promise Zones, as well as many other programs in the state. (A similar demonstration effect can be seen in the Arkansas cluster, where neighboring communities were inspired to emulate the El Dorado Promise.) But more important is the fact that urban communities in the nation's older population centers face similar challenges, among them depopulation, falling school district enrollment, and declining home prices, which make them less able to retain residents and businesses. By offering a strategy to make a place more attractive, the Promise model has drawn the attention of leaders in all kinds of struggling communities.

More specifically, the Promise model seeks to address two problems plaguing communities of many sizes and types: educational outcomes and economic performance. For decades, policymakers at all levels of government have experimented with approaches to increase educational attainment and improve economic competitiveness. Statewide merit aid programs are one example, as they are designed not only to reward academic performance in high school and increase access to higher education but also to retain college-educated workers in-state to aid economic competitiveness. They are also an excellent example of policy diffusion, with 25 states introducing such programs between 1991 and 2004 (Sjoquist and Winters 2014). Cities, too, especially those in the industrial regions of the Northeast and upper Midwest, have struggled to address these twin goals of economic revitalization and educational opportunity. Often these priorities are traded off against each other, with taxpayers, policymakers, and philanthropists asked to allocate scarce resources to one or the other. The Kalamazoo Promise represented an unprecedented merging of these two priorities. Whether consciously or not, the message of the donors, widely believed to include prominent Kalamazoo business people, was that you cannot have one without the other—that only by investing in education and, more specifically, in the public school district that serves the urban core, can the community remain economically competitive.

This message resonated in communities across the nation facing similar challenges: by supporting and encouraging higher education for local youth, not only can we increase the human capital of our residents, but we can also make ourselves more competitive economically, more attractive to new business and residents, and better able to hold onto those already here.

HOW DID THE PLACE-BASED SCHOLARSHIP MODEL SPREAD?

Whatever the attributes of the Kalamazoo Promise, its diffusion would have been highly unlikely if the national media had not widely reported on its introduction of the Kalamazoo Promise. There are several reasons for the intensity of the media coverage in the wake of the announcement. First, the Promise was indeed a new idea. It represented the first time that a scholarship had been made available for nearly every graduate of a sizable school district. Second, the generous terms of the program—full tuition and fees at any public university or college in Michigan, awarded on a first-dollar basis, guaranteed in perpetuity, and financed by private dollars—attracted a great deal of attention, as did the intriguing question of the anonymous donors. Who were they? Would their names be revealed? What motivated their giving? Much of the mainstream media played up the human interest angle—the Kalamazoo Promise as a life-changing opportunity for low-income youth in a city still reeling from the loss of its major employer, the Upjohn Company (a pharmaceutical firm that merged with Pharmacia and was later acquired by Pfizer, sending hundreds of high-level jobs out of the area), as well as the closing of a General Motors auto plant and the demise of a formerly robust paper industry. Meanwhile, the economic revitalization implications attracted the attention of more serious news outlets, including the *Wall Street Journal*, the *New York Times*, and the *Economist*, especially because the stimulus was coming from private rather than taxpayer dollars.

The value of the Promise concept was reinforced by a series of national awards, such as those from *Fast Company* magazine (2007), which included Kalamazoo in its sixth Annual Fast 50 (portraits of "people and businesses writing the history of the next 10 years") and America's Promise, an alliance for youth, which repeatedly rated Kalamazoo as one of the nation's "100 Best Communities for Young People" despite child poverty rates that are among the highest in the country (Jessup 2007). The program was also recognized by more specialized organizations, such as Partners for Livable Communities, which chose Kalamazoo as one of three cities to receive its 2006 Entrepreneurial American Leadership Award, and *Expansion Management* magazine, which included the metropolitan area on its Five-Star Quality of Life Metros list (Chourey [2006]; see Miller-Adams [2009a, pp. 188–189] for more details). While such honors may have gone unnoticed by the general public, they drew attention to Kalamazoo within business and policy circles, and have been recognized and embraced by economic development officials as marketing tools with which to promote the community and attract new business to the region.

Media coverage, as well as interpersonal communication, was critical to the diffusion of the Promise model, as the following examples suggest.

- In El Dorado, a member of the local chamber of commerce brought a news article about the Kalamazoo Promise to a chamber meeting in the spring of 2006, a few months after the program was announced. Excited by the idea (at that time, no results had been reported), local citizens approached the city's largest employer, Murphy Oil Corporation, which had long been a supporter of education in this community. The company's CEO, Claiborne Deming, sent a team to Kalamazoo to learn more. The El Dorado Promise was launched in January 2007 with a $50 million gift from Murphy Oil. Modeled closely on the Kalamazoo Promise, its terms are the most generous of any Promise program.[1]

- In Denver, Bernadette Marquez, a Kalamazoo-area native, heard about the Kalamazoo Promise from family members still living in the area. She and her husband, Tim Marquez, then chairman of oil producer Venoco, worked with the mayor and school superintendent to create a place-based scholarship program for Denver Public Schools. The Denver Scholarship Foundation, launched with a $50 million challenge grant from the Marquezes, provides college access support to all students in the district while awarding needs-based tuition scholarships to most graduates of the public school system.[2]

- Pittsburgh Public Schools Superintendent Mark Roosevelt was two months into his new job, dealing with a rapidly shrinking school district and closing schools, when he read about the Kalamazoo Promise. He spent 10 months speaking with people privately about a Pittsburgh Promise and its potential to reverse negative trends under way in the district, finally teaming up with new mayor Luke Ravenstahl, only 27 years old at the time. The two made an audacious decision to announce their intention to create a similar program before they had any funding in hand. Their December 2006 announcement met with skepticism that evaporated a year later when the University of Pittsburgh Medical Center, the city's largest employer, committed $100 million in challenge grant funding to support the program (Hamill 2008).

These three programs, like the Kalamazoo Promise, originated in private conversations with individuals marshaling their resources and building alliances to create place-based scholarships in their own communities. This has been the prevailing mechanism through which the Promise model has spread nationally. However, a second important mechanism of diffusion followed a very different path.

The Michigan Promise Zones are a public policy innovation introduced by the administration of Governor Jennifer Granholm and are a further example of the process of reinvention. In 2006, Governor Granholm's communications and policy adviser, Chuck Wilbur, began visiting Kalamazoo and speaking with people about how the

Kalamazoo Promise might be emulated statewide. With the governor's support, and working with several key legislators, Wilbur devised a unique public–private partnership model that took into account the terrible condition of Michigan's public finances at the time. Promise Zones are funded through three sources: 1) individual students' need-based aid (including Pell Grants); 2) money raised from private (generally local) sources; and 3) in their third year of operation, a portion of the State Education Tax captured through a tax-increment financing structure. Promise Zones legislation was introduced in 2007 and signed into law in 2009. By 2013, 8 of the 10 Promise Zone communities were granting scholarships.[3]

The Promise Zones effort dovetailed with a second education-related initiative of the Granholm administration, the creation of the Michigan College Access Network, which was modeled on a similar initiative in Ohio. Through this initiative, federal and foundation grants were accessed to help support the creation of local college access networks throughout the state. Before the governor left office, the Michigan College Access Network became an independent nonprofit providing seed funding and technical assistance to communities seeking to organize their college access efforts. Over 40 local college access networks were in place in mid-2015, many of which work with Promise scholarship programs in their local communities. The combined impact of the Kalamazoo Promise, Michigan Promise Zones, and the Michigan College Access Network has made the state a leader in college-access efforts nationwide.

PROMISE EFFORTS THAT DID NOT SUCCEED

Not every effort to replicate the Kalamazoo Promise has been successful. The following stories suggest that money, politics, and community support all play a role in the successful launch of a place-based scholarship program.

- Newton, Iowa, was one of the earliest communities to consider a Promise program, beginning discussions only a few months after the Kalamazoo program was announced. Planning was spearheaded by the Newton Economic Development Corporation in response to the impending departure of the Maytag Corporation, the city's major employer. A planning group met for several years, but resistance to using public monies as part of the funding structure, along with the departure from the community of a key advocate, ultimately doomed the effort.[4]

- In Flint, Michigan, a roundtable of potential funders convened shortly after the announcement of the Kalamazoo Promise, evolving into the Greater Flint Education Exploratory Committee, a task group of educators, foundation officials, and business representatives that met regularly for several years. The group ultimately concluded that the community did not have the financial resources for a Flint Promise. The deeply distressed condition of the local economy and lack of participation by the city (a key player in many Promise communities) also shaped the final outcome. Flint has continued to explore the place-based scholarship model, with its state legislators seeking to expand the number of authorized Promise Zones so that a Flint Promise might be created (Schuch 2014).

- In Davenport, Iowa, a task force of city, school, and community leaders led the push to provide scholarships through a reallocation of proceeds from the city's $0.01 local-option sales tax. Despite a deliberate convening process, which included multiple public consultations, extensive media coverage, and the commissioning of an economic impact study, the program failed when it was put to a vote in a special election in March 2009. Proponents blamed the harsh economic climate, although an organized opposition that insisted such a program be privately funded was clearly a factor.

- Another program that met defeat at the ballot box was in Akron, Ohio, where the mayor proposed to pay for a Promise scholarship through the privatization of the city's sewer system. Inspired by both the Kalamazoo Promise and the trend toward privatizing public services, the city sought the financial advice of investment bank Morgan Stanley and set up an advisory group to study the transaction and recommend key terms. The deal put before voters in November 2008 called for the lease of the sewer system for an up-front payment of $250 million, which would be used to create an endowment to support a scholarship program for Akron students. The proposed program was more restrictive and less generous than those on which it was modeled; while scholarships would be available to all high school graduates, they could be used only at local institutions. And the legislation included a controversial provision requiring recipients to continue to pay the city's income tax for 30 years, even if they were to leave Akron. The ballot initiative drew vocal opposition from a group of residents who formed a grass roots organization to lobby against it and was defeated by a large margin (63 percent opposed to 37 percent in favor). Most of the opposition centered on the privatization of public services, but critical to the debate was the perception that the mayor had developed his plan without broad public input.[5]

It is difficult to generalize about what accounts for success and failure when it comes to developing Promise programs. All of these communities had "champions," an individual or group of committed leaders to spearhead the initiative, and all but Akron made serious efforts to marshal community support for the planning effort. Funding was a challenge in all four cases, but this is true for most successful Promise efforts as well. Ultimately, these stories suggest that without strong stakeholder support and buy-in, the financial resources needed to support a Promise program will be difficult to obtain. They also underscore the particular challenge of accessing public funds for

Promise scholarships. To date, the Promise movement remains essentially a privately funded innovation.

BUILDING A NETWORK

While there is no formal coordinator of Promise programs, a robust informal network exists among individuals involved in such initiatives. The story of the creation of this network underscores Rogers's (2003) emphasis on interpersonal communication and is a stellar example of how communities can learn from each other even in the absence of central leadership.

As leaders in other communities began thinking about whether and how to create Promise programs, many of them visited Kalamazoo (often as a group) to meet with school officials, the Kalamazoo Promise administrator, economic development practitioners, and local researchers. Many others spent time learning about the program through phone conversations or e-mail exchanges. Representatives from Kalamazoo were invited to visit other communities and speak with planning groups. With growing awareness of national interest in the Promise model, in December 2007 the W.E. Upjohn Institute for Employment Research convened a group of individuals from seven communities to assess the expansion of the movement and discuss the possibility of organizing a meeting at which information about the place-based scholarship approach could be shared more efficiently. The result was the inaugural meeting of PromiseNet, held in Kalamazoo in June 2008.

The first PromiseNet conference, which planners had expected to attract 50 attendees, ultimately drew over 200 participants from 30 states. All the nation's regions were represented, with attendees coming from large cities (including Denver, Cleveland, Pittsburgh, and San Francisco), rural communities, and everywhere in between. Interestingly, the invitation list was simply a compilation of the names of people who had contacted or visited Kalamazoo over the previous few years, suggesting that the interpersonal communications channels that evolved following the introduction of the Kalamazoo Promise had become remarkably broad. The conference itself brought about a new round of media coverage, and within days of its conclusion, other communities organizing Promise programs or considering their development had surfaced. This time, the focus of media reports was not on the Kalamazoo Promise per se, but on the movement it had sparked.

Efforts to bring Promise communities together have continued, although in the same kind of ad hoc way that the programs themselves have emerged. No one is in charge of PromiseNet; it has no office, no staff, and no financial resources. Communities step forward and announce their intention to host. Kalamazoo has done so four times (2008, 2010, 2013, 2015), with the 2015 meeting coinciding with the tenth anniversary of the announcement of the Kalamazoo Promise. Denver, Pittsburgh, and New Haven have also hosted PromiseNet meetings. The conferences are planned by volunteers representing multiple Promise communities; the host community takes it upon itself to procure local corporate support or in-kind donations, and a modest conference fee is charged to individual participants. The emphasis of past conferences has been on networking and mutual learning, with the agenda usually determined by input from those planning to attend.

There have been sporadic initiatives to link Promise communities more closely, including a short-lived listserv and occasional conversations at PromiseNet conferences about the future of the network. The most formal of these discussions was a town hall meeting at PromiseNet 2014, organized by the New Haven Promise and held at Yale University's School of Organization and Management (SOM). The session was built around a case study written by Yale SOM staff entitled *PromiseNet: Toward a More Unified Network?* (Wiggins 2014). Despite prompting by the session's organizers and facilitator, neither the panelists (who represented the leadership of four established Promise programs and one researcher) nor those audience members who spoke concluded that a more formal network was needed. The reasons for their reluctance varied. Some participants noted that information about how to launch a Promise program is already available through informal networking, PromiseNet conferences, and consulting services available from the W.E. Upjohn Institute for Employment Research, RAND Corporation, McKinsey & Company, and university-based evaluators. Others emphasized the diversity of program structure and need for communities to be responsive to the local context. The most passionate comments came from Pittsburgh Promise Executive Director Saleem Ghubril, who made the case that Promise leaders must focus above all on serving the children of their community, and that any effort that takes time, energy, or financial resources away from that core endeavor is a distraction.

Despite a reluctance to organize more formally, Promise communities remain connected through both interpersonal ties among stakeholders, the cross-fertilization of ideas, and a relationship among researchers that has been built over the past several years. The Upjohn Institute hosts a Promise-related section on its website that brings together its own research with that of others working in the field. Researchers from multiple communities meet at various academic conferences where Promise programs have been the focus of numerous sessions. In 2014, the research effort got a boost from the Lumina Foundation, the Indianapolis-based philanthropy whose mission is to promote increased rates of postsecondary attainment. In 2013, Lumina and the Upjohn Institute cohosted a meeting for Promise researchers from 16 communities. Based on this effort, the Promise Research Consortium was formed in 2014 and a two-year integrated research program launched. Among the expected results of this initiative are comparative findings about the impact of Promise programs on postsecondary attainment across multiple communities, a website where new Promise communities can learn about best practices (Promisenet.net), and information about indicators that Promise stakeholders can use to analyze their own programs. The research community is hopeful that more solid empirical evidence about the impact of Promise programs on local school districts, postsecondary outcomes, and community development will become available through efforts like this one, making true learning possible.

The Promise model has proven robust, with new programs being announced regularly and many more in the planning phase. There are almost as many versions of Promise programs as there are programs themselves; however, the fundamental features of the Kalamazoo Promise have remained intact throughout the diffusion process. These include the place-based structure that limits the awarding of scholarships to a given school district or city; a sliding scale of benefits designed to reward continuous residency and enrollment; and a lengthy duration, reflecting an understanding of the long-term nature of the changes resulting from the program. In the next chapter, I turn to the critical distinctions among Promise programs and assess which features matter most.

Notes

1. See the El Dorado Promise website: http://www.eldoradopromise.com (accessed July 30, 2015).
2. See the Denver Scholarship Foundation website: http://www.denver scholarship.org/ (accessed July 30, 2015).
3. See PromiseZones.org (accessed July 30, 2015). In July 2015, the Jackson Promise Zone dissolved, bringing the number of Promise Zones to nine.
4. Personal communication with Kim Didier, executive director, Newton Development Corporation.
5. As this book was going to press, basketball superstar LeBron James announced a scholarship for low-income students in partnership with the University of Akron that could benefit up to 2,300 Akron public school graduates (Schleis 2015).

Chapter 4

Not All Promise Programs Are Alike—Does It Matter?

Media coverage of the Kalamazoo Promise following its November 2005 announcement stimulated conversations in many communities about whether and how to replicate the program. The results were almost immediate, with seven communities establishing place-based scholarship programs in 2006 alone. (Many other communities began planning processes at the time, some of which resulted in Promise programs introduced in subsequent years.) This initial period was critically important in the evolution of the Promise movement; while all these programs were inspired by the Kalamazoo Promise, they differed in their approaches, and each new model became a template available to future Promise efforts.

Among the place-based scholarship programs announced in 2006 were four programs that retained the universal eligibility characteristics of the Kalamazoo Promise but limited attendance to the local community college. The genesis of each was slightly different, with the Peoria Promise (Illinois) initiated by the mayor, the Ventura College Promise (California) by the local community college, the Jackson Legacy (Michigan) by the community foundation, and the Garrett County Scholarship Program (Maryland) by the county commissioners. A fifth such program, the Legacy Scholars in Battle Creek, had been created in 2005 by the W.K. Kellogg Foundation as part of its 75th anniversary celebration and predates the Kalamazoo Promise by only a few days.

Also in 2006, the Denver Scholarship Foundation announced its needs-based approach as part of a pilot program in three high schools (expanded to the entire district in 2008), and the Pittsburgh Promise introduced its merit-based model. Finally, the city of Hammond (Indiana) created a program to meet its own critical need—increasing home ownership in this declining industrial city just south of Chicago—by awarding full-tuition scholarships to the children of homeowners who meet strict merit criteria.[1]

This group of early adopters captured key variations in two of the most critical elements of Promise program design: which students are eligible for the scholarship, and which institutions can they attend. Table 4.1 summarizes these distinctions for the population of Promise programs created in the two years after the Kalamazoo Promise was announced.

The steady growth in the number of place-based scholarship programs in the intervening years has taken place without a single model coming to dominate. As Table 4.2 shows, of the approximately 50 programs granting scholarships in 2015, about half allow students a wide choice of postsecondary institutions, while the others restrict attendance to one or more local institutions. Similarly, about half of the existing programs incorporate the universal eligibility provision introduced by the Kalamazoo Promise. Most of the others have

Table 4.1 Promise Programs in 2007

Expansive	
Universal	Limited[a]
Kalamazoo Promise	College Bound
El Dorado Promise	Denver Scholarship Foundation
Northport Promise	Pittsburgh Promise

Restrictive	
Universal	Limited[a]
Peoria Promise	Tulsa Achieves
Ventura College Promise	Bay Commitment
Garrett County Scholarship Program	
Jackson Legacy	
Legacy Scholars	

NOTE: Programs that limit postsecondary attendance to one or more local or regional institutions are labeled restrictive, while those that provide more geographic options are labeled expansive.

[a] Dependent on academic merit, financial need, or other requirements.

Table 4.2 Promise Programs in 2015

Expansive	
Universal	Limited[a]
Baldwin Promise[a]	Arkadelphia Promise
Benton Harbor Promise[a]	Challenge Scholars[b]
CORE Promise Scholarship	Cleveland County Promise
El Dorado Promise	College Bound
Hazel Park Promise[a]	Denver Scholarship Foundation
Kalamazoo Promise	Hartford Promise[b]
Pontiac Promise[a]	Holland-Zeeland Promise
Rockford Promise	La Crosse Promise[b]
Saginaw Promise[a]	New Haven Promise
Say Yes Buffalo	Northport Promise
Say Yes Syracuse	Pittsburgh Promise
Tangelo Park Program	
tnAchieves	
Restrictive	
Universal	Limited[a]
Battle Creek Promise[a]	Bay Commitment
Detroit Scholarship Fund[a]	Chicago Star Scholarship
Dyer County Promise	College Promise
Educate and Grow[b]	Harper College Promise[b]
Galesburg Promise	H.O.P.E. Scholarship
Garrett County Scholarship Program	Hopkinsville Rotary Scholars
Great River Promise	Jackson Legacy
Lansing Promise[a]	Montgomery County Ohio
Legacy Scholars	College Promise
Long Beach College Promise	Partners Advancing College
Pensacola Pledge Scholars	Education (PACE)
Ventura College Promise	Peoria Promise
	Promise for the Future
	Rochester Promise
	Rusk TJC Citizens Promise
	School Counts!
	Tulsa Achieves

NOTE: Programs that limit postsecondary attendance to one or more local or regional institutions are labeled restrictive, while those that provide more geographic options are labeled expansive.

[a] Michigan Promise Zone.

[b] Program announced but not awarding scholarships. See Appendix A for more information.

adopted merit requirements that include a minimum GPA and attendance rate, along with service or other requirements. In a few cases,
there are both merit and need requirements; for example, students
must have a 2.0 GPA and exhibit financial need to receive support
through the Denver Scholarship Foundation. (One of the mysteries of
the Promise movement is that so few programs target their scholarships toward low-income students. This suggests that statewide merit
aid programs are at least as powerful a model for local Promise programs as is the Kalamazoo Promise.)[2]

This chapter addresses these two key design questions, briefly
touching on the question of eligible postsecondary institutions and
then focusing on the choice of a universal or targeted model when it
comes to student eligibility.[3]

WHERE CAN PROMISE STUDENTS GO TO COLLEGE?

There is tremendous variety within the population of Promise
programs when it comes to use of the scholarship. The El Dorado
Promise, for example, allows recipients to take their scholarships
(capped at the highest in-state tuition rate for a public institution) to
any accredited postsecondary institution in the nation, while the Long
Beach College Promise provides one semester of tuition at the local
community college. It is relatively easy to distinguish between the
most flexible and most restrictive programs, especially as there is a
large group of programs that cover only a single two-year institution.
The challenge lies in deciding how to categorize those programs that
fall in between. For purposes of this research, programs that limit
postsecondary attendance to one or more local or regional institutions are labeled restrictive, while those that provide more geographic
options are labeled expansive. For example, the Detroit Scholarship
Fund, which allows graduates of Detroit Public Schools to attend one
of five regional community colleges, falls into the restrictive category.

(In this usage, the term *restrictive* refers to postsecondary options, not the generosity of the funding itself.)

In contrast to stakeholder decisions about student eligibility (discussed below), the choice of postsecondary options has been largely driven by cost. The least expensive way to create a Promise program is to limit attendance to community college, where the cost of tuition is well below that of four-year schools, and make it a "last-dollar" program—that is, the Promise scholarship is awarded after other forms of financial aid. For school districts where a high proportion of students qualify for free- or reduced-price meals and thus are eligible for some level of Pell Grant funding, this program structure will reduce the cost of the Promise program dramatically because, in almost every state, Pell Grants more than cover the cost of tuition and fees at community colleges. (If the program is structured as a first-dollar scholarship or allows expenses beyond tuition and fees to be covered, its costs will be higher.)

One can legitimately ask whether a last-dollar, community college program for a high-poverty school district actually has any impact. Students graduating from that district qualify for Pell Grants and thus can already attend community college for free (provided they complete their FAFSA). While there is limited research on this question, some Promise programs have reported a boost in college-going, possibly due to the greater simplicity of messaging that the program makes possible.[4]

Promise programs that restrict attendance to local community colleges can be a good choice for communities concerned with workforce development, since students who attend local postsecondary institutions are more likely to remain in the local community after graduation than those who attend college outside the area. A "local institution only" program also makes possible close coordination between the K–12 district and the postsecondary institution; community colleges historically receive many students from the local school district and are familiar with the barriers students face and types of remediation required. Community colleges provide valuable benefits not only to lower-achieving students who might not have gone to college in the absence of a Promise program but also to more academically prepared students who can transfer to a four-year institution with two years of free coursework toward a bachelor's degree.

Finally, "community college only" programs effectively target low-income students while remaining open to everyone. Because of their lower levels of academic readiness, low-income students are more likely than middle- or upper-income students to attend two-year institutions. These programs also address the concerns of stakeholders worried about extending a tuition benefit to someone who is already on a college-going track, as such programs do not tend to attract the better-prepared student who is already bound for a four-year institution. The career and technical education offerings of community colleges, including short-term certificate programs and in some cases apprenticeship programs, can provide a meaningful financial boost to a student who would otherwise face limited job opportunities with only a high school degree. However, the challenge of accomplishing this is high, as two-year institutions tend to be underresourced, and the students who attend them have the greatest need of remediation.

Ideally, stakeholder decisions about eligible postsecondary institutions will be driven by a community's critical need rather than cost alone. In reality, communities with limited financial resources may opt for a low-cost program to ensure that their Promise is sustainable. While the transformative potential of such a program is more limited than that of a more generous or flexible program, it can still be an effective way to reduce barriers to higher education for low-income students, contribute to local workforce needs, and strengthen the college-going culture of a school district.

While stakeholder decisions about eligible postsecondary institutions often reflect cost concerns, such concerns are not the sole motivation for limiting student eligibility. What factors, other than cost, have led so many Promise programs to reject the universal eligibility provision of the Kalamazoo Promise?

THE UNIVERSAL VERSUS TARGETED DEBATE

Social scientists and policymakers have long debated whether social programs are most effective if they are designed to reach an entire population or targeted toward a specific group. There is an extensive literature weighing the pros and cons of these two approaches, covering topics as diverse as school lunches, telephone service, and old-age pensions. To summarize its findings, universal programs are generally seen as more feasible, more likely to reach all segments of the highest-need population, and nonstigmatizing. Targeted programs, on the other hand, are usually considered more efficient in that they distribute scarce resources to the population that needs or deserves them the most (Vaade and McCready 2011).

Social programs are most often targeted based on financial need. Head Start, federally subsidized school meals, the Supplemental Nutrition Assistance or Food Stamp Program, housing vouchers, and Medicaid all go to families below a given income level. The largest category of student financial aid (not counting loans)—federal Pell Grants—also conforms to this model. But there is a competing approach to financial aid that has become increasingly important in recent decades: statewide merit-based aid programs, such as the Georgia Hope Scholarship. Since 1991, more than two dozen states have introduced broad merit-based scholarship programs available to all residents who meet certain criteria, usually a minimum GPA of 3.0 in high school and sometimes a minimum score on a college-entrance exam. The scholarships are generally awarded to students regardless of family income and are designed to increase college access and attainment, reward strong academic performance, and keep the best students in-state for their college years.

Assessments of the impact of these programs on college access vary, with some scholars arguing that they mainly benefit students who would attend college in any case (Cornwell, Mustard, and Sridhar 2006; Heller 2006), and others arguing that they have had a positive impact in shifting students from two-year to four-year schools (Dynarski 2004). The impact on college completion is debated as well, with some scholars finding that state merit aid programs have had no meaningful positive effect on college completion (Sjoquist and Winters 2014) and others seeing positive effects (see Scott-Clayton [2011] regarding the West Virginia Promise).

A few Promise programs target their scholarships to students with financial need, but most are modeled more closely on merit aid programs with resources available only for the more successful students and scholarship programs designed at least in part to promote higher achievement in the K–12 system.

The Pittsburgh Promise was the first of the merit-based programs and has become a powerful model for other communities. The Pittsburgh story is instructive not only to see how and why this model originated, but also because the path to its creation was quite different from what transpired in Kalamazoo.

The Kalamazoo Promise was developed in private by a small group of individuals and then unveiled to the broader community with full funding in place. In Pittsburgh, the reverse was the case. In December 2006, when the mayor and school superintendent announced that there would be a Pittsburgh Promise, the program had no structure, no substance, and no money. While many welcomed the news, there was skepticism about whether a scholarship program would ever come to pass, as well as frustration on the part of some that its premature announcement would damage the program's future prospects.

Details were worked out over the subsequent 12 months with a stakeholder engagement process that included a report from a national consulting firm, intensive discussions among community leaders, and negotiations with the University of Pittsburgh Medical Center, which was approached to become the program's lead funder. The original vision of the superintendent was reportedly not one of a merit-based program; in his initial announcement, just over a year after the Kalamazoo Promise was introduced, he commented that he did not envision any kind of GPA requirement. "What we will be saying to kids in the Pittsburgh Public Schools is, if you play by the rules, and you do what you're supposed to do, and you do your work, and you graduate . . . there will be education after high school in your future, and money will not be what holds you back" (Lord 2006). An outside consulting firm hired to explore program structure options also seemed to advocate a program that would reach as many students as possible, noting among its five design principles that "broadly accessible eligibility requirements create confidence that the Promise will benefit most students" (McKinsey & Company 2007, p. 5). Yet during the year-long engagement process, community leaders decided that a minimum GPA and strict attendance policy would best serve their purposes.

Members of the stakeholder group acknowledge that money was a concern, but that context was more important in opting for a merit requirement. The school superintendent at the time had been hired in 2005 with a mandate to bring about school reform. In his first year, he had presided over the closing of 30 schools (and the opening of 4), all with an eye to improving the performance of the school district. In designing the Pittsburgh Promise, stakeholders felt compelled to embrace this drive for reform and the creation of a culture of high expectations. The group wrestled with whether or not to follow the Kalamazoo Promise's universal eligibility model or impose some academic requirements. Ultimately, informed by research that connects GPA with college persistence, the group opted for a 2.5 cutoff as the appropriate level. There was concern, however, that this was not fair to students already in the system who would not have time to increase their GPA to this level, so the group reached a compromise that would scale up the GPA and attendance requirements (2.0 to 2.5 and 85 percent to 90 percent, respectively) over the first few years of the program.

For students who fall below the 2.5 GPA cutoff but have higher than a C average—approximately one-quarter of graduating seniors—there is a "Promise Extension" program that pays for attendance at the local community college for a year. If students are successful at maintaining a 2.0 GPA in that setting, they become eligible to receive full funding and use it at any of the schools covered by the Pittsburgh Promise. While the Promise Extension is publicized in the high schools by guidance counselors and Pittsburgh Promise outreach staff, it is not mentioned on the website, in line with efforts to encourage students to aspire to the 2.5 GPA level.

A more recent program change announced in June 2014 allows students to access Pittsburgh Promise funding while still in high school to attend select career and technology programs at the local community college. Most Promise programs cover career and technical education when it is offered by eligible institutions, but for students in college, not high school. Evidence suggests, however, that many of the students who could benefit from this kind of practical training for in-demand jobs drop out of high school before being able to take advantage of Promise funding. Pittsburgh's effort seeks to short-circuit this pattern, engaging students in career paths while they are still in high school. Students participating in the program can graduate from high school with as many as 24 postsecondary credits, up to four workforce certifications, a driver's license, and soft-skills training. Additionally, if they choose to go on for further education, they will still have Promise funding remaining. Notably, there are no GPA or attendance requirements for participation in this program (Chute 2014).

Both the Promise Extension program and the high school technical training program, as well as a recently announced mentoring initiative for black males (Chute 2015), suggest that Pittsburgh Promise stakeholders are seeking to reach more students through creative strategies that soften the merit requirements in place for the traditional Pittsburgh Promise program.

CHOOSING A MODEL

A Merit-Based Approach

After 2007, the designers of Promise programs had an important choice to make: Should they emulate the universal eligibility provisions of the Kalamazoo Promise, or should they follow Pittsburgh in requiring students to meet academic and behavioral standards in order to receive the scholarship? A third choice, making scholarships contingent on financial need, as was done in Denver, was also on the table, but few Promise stakeholders pursued this approach.[5]

In a study of postsecondary opportunity programs, researchers at the University of Wisconsin asked program designers about the targeted versus universal decision (Vaade and McCready 2011). Most respondents said that cost considerations were not driving their decision to limit scholarships to more academically successful students. Although cost may play more of a role than respondents claim, other factors, such as a desire to prepare students adequately for success in college and an interest in limiting scholarships to worthy recipients, are also clearly involved. Stakeholders in communities that have adopted merit criteria for their Promise programs are seeking two interrelated outcomes: 1) the creation of a climate of high expectations and improved achievement in the K–12 setting, and 2) adequate preparation of students for college success. (Some may also be pursuing the community-level goal mentioned earlier of attracting residents who value education.) The first set of academic goals seeks to use the carrot of a merit-based scholarship to encourage students to work harder and be more responsible in high school in order to gain a valuable financial resource. The limited evidence to date, however, does not show achievement levels rising in response to merit-based programs.

The college preparedness argument is more convincing. Progression and retention data from national sources show that many students who go to college struggle to complete their degrees; this problem is most acute at the community college level, where open-admission rules prevail. For students who are not adequately prepared for post-secondary education, the experience of failure can have a negative psychological impact, damaging self-esteem and deterring any interest in further academic experiences. The National Center for Education Statistics (NCES) reports that 59 percent of first-time, full-time students who began seeking a bachelor's degree at a four-year institution in fall 2006 completed the degree at that institution within six years (U.S. Department of Education 2014).[6] At community colleges, NCES reports a 31 percent completion rate within three years for full-time, first-time undergraduate students who began their pursuit of a certificate or an associate's degree in fall 2008. Alternative success measures that include the proportion of community college students transferring to four-year institutions increase this rate to around 40 percent, still well below the rate for those entering four-year institutions directly.

Some Promise stakeholders worry that the Promise model emphasizes college access over college success. They note that students who are not academically prepared for higher education may spend their Promise funds without accumulating credits, depleting their funding before completing a degree. (This is a major concern for universal programs, where low-achieving students can attend open-admission institutions and may use up part of their scholarships taking non-credit-bearing remedial courses.) Merit requirements ensure that only those students who are at the higher end of the academic achievement continuum will have access to the scholarship, while attendance requirements are a proxy for responsible behavior and a strong work ethic, two other critical elements in college success. Pittsburgh's Promise Extension program is a creative solution to encourage students at the margin to attempt higher education in a community college setting, but it does nothing for students with cumulative GPAs below a C level. Only universal programs offer something to those students.

A final line of reasoning—that students should be required to earn their scholarships through good grades and by meeting certain behavioral standards—is harder to parse, as it reflects deep-seated beliefs about meritocracy and discomfort with the notion of giving money to low-achieving students. This point of view, however, neglects the incentives and accountability mechanism built into most Promise programs, whether universal or merit-based (except for those that offer a fixed amount of funding). Students may use their scholarships only at a higher education institution to which they have been admitted. In the case of the Kalamazoo Promise, if you are an excellent student and can gain admission to the University of Michigan (the state's most competitive institution) or one of the private colleges that have recently joined the list of eligible institutions, your scholarship will be worth between $57,000 and $170,000 over four years based on current tuition rates. If, on the other hand, you are a struggling student with a poor GPA but you manage to graduate from high school, you can attend one of the state's open-admissions community colleges where your scholarship will be worth, on average, between $2,000 and $3,000 a year. The same is true for many other Promise programs in which higher tuition awards coincide with more selective institutions. (It is worth noting that for-profit colleges are generally not included among eligible institutions for Promise scholarships; these entities are known for targeting students who have financial aid resources for enrolling, then failing to adequately support their success once in college.)

The drawbacks of a merit-based Promise program structure are highlighted by how hard it is to determine what the appropriate merit cutoff should be. The minimum GPA required by various Promise programs ranges from 2.0 (Denver) to 2.5 (Pittsburgh Promise and others) to 3.0 (New Haven and Hartford). Communities grappling with where to draw the line should ensure that decisions about merit cutoffs are based not just on the instincts of stakeholders but on the critical need a community is seeking to address and real evidence of impact.

A Universal Approach

Given what is known about the goals of Promise programs—increasing access to higher education, inspiring cultural change in the K–12 system, and transforming communities—there is a strong case to be made for universal eligibility. The following features of universal programs are especially important.

School culture. Most Promise programs include among their goals the creation or strengthening of the college-going culture of the K–12 district. Critical to this discussion is the notion that "college" encompasses not just four-year bachelor's degree programs but also shorter associate's degrees and career and technical education certification offered by community colleges. In the case of a universal program, virtually every student in the district is a potential beneficiary of the scholarship; in Kalamazoo, for example, 95 percent of graduates are eligible for Kalamazoo Promise funding. This means that efforts to promote a college-going culture have the potential to resonate with the entire student body. It is more difficult to leverage a Promise scholarship for cultural change in a district where merit-based requirements are in place. In New Haven, for example, less than one-third of high school graduates are eligible for the New Haven Promise. In Pittsburgh, where the GPA threshold is a bit lower, around 70 percent of high school seniors qualify when you include the Promise Extension. Cultural change is never easy, but it is simpler in a setting where everyone believes they have the same or similar opportunities.

College readiness. One of the most powerful arguments made by advocates of GPA requirements is that Promise scholarships are not just about college access but also college success, and that students below a certain GPA are not likely to be successful in the more rigorous environment of a postsecondary institution. This argument often neglects the fact that virtually every Promise program provides funding for career and technical training programs offered by community colleges, and some allow Promise funds to be used for apprenticeship or other trades programs. As a rule, these programs do not require high GPAs or test scores (although they often have math and reading proficiency requirements), yet they provide important paths to certificates and associate's degrees that can dramatically increase an individual's earnings. Another shortcoming of the college readiness argument is that people change over time; many individuals who struggle in high school because they lack motivation or direction excel later on once their interests and passions are engaged. Cutting these students out of a merit-based scholarship program unnecessarily limits the return on the human capital investment represented by the Promise program.

Simplicity. As I have discussed elsewhere, simplicity of program structure is one of the hallmarks of the Kalamazoo Promise and arguably one of the reasons it has been replicated (and reinvented) in so many different ways (Miller-Adams 2009b). This simplicity has also been a valuable asset to those operating the program, aiding in communication with internal and external audiences and keeping administrative costs to a minimum. The very few requirements for receiving the scholarship and the ease of filling out its one-page application have helped Kalamazoo Promise administrators and school officials communicate the program's rules to K–12 students and their families, as well as encourage participation. In Promise communities with more complex programs, the task of communication is more difficult, and the bar for getting students and families to sign up is higher. The simple program structure has also been helpful in external messaging or branding of the Kalamazoo community. It is relatively easy to explain to outsiders the terms of the program and to promote the notion of Kalamazoo as an "Education Community." A further benefit is that administrative costs are low; as noted earlier, a single administrator operated all aspects of the program for almost three years, and the staff now consists of two full-time employees and one or two interns. A final advantage of simplicity is the issue of appeals. Every program rule gives rise to a certain number of appeals from students and families who feel like their unique circumstances warrant special attention. In the case of Kalamazoo, these appeals center on the program's only requirements: continuous residency and enrollment. But even these have required the creation of an appeals board that hears from an average of 40 students each year. Programs with more complex rules generate more appeals, which in turn adds to the time and cost of administering the program.

Serving low-income and minority students. The achievement gaps that run along racial and income lines throughout most K–12 systems means that low-income and minority students are overrepresented in that portion of the student body that cannot gain admission to four-year, competitive-admission institutions. For these students, attendance at a community college offers the best—and sometimes the only—path to gainful employment, whether through a short-term career or technical training program, or an associate's degree (and possible transfer to a four-year institution). By limiting use of scholarship dollars to students above a certain GPA threshold, Promise programs are cutting out of the picture those students who are not able to gain admission to four-year institutions, many of whom are racial/ethnic minorities or low-income, first-generation college-goers.

Strength of incentive. Promise programs' emphasis on community transformation sets them apart from the general field of financial aid. To accomplish this, programs must create incentives for families with school-age children to move to or remain within the local community. Universal programs offer what is in effect a larger and more flexible carrot to families who may be considering a move. But for families with young children (or whose children are not even born yet), scholarships that will be awarded 10, 15, or 20 years down the road are worth less than those awarded today—intervening events, such as a job loss requiring relocation, may negate the value of the scholarship (a phenomenon known in economics as the discount rate). If parents must also calculate what kind of student their child will be—for example, what kind of grades or attendance record he or she will have—this makes the discount rate even steeper. An open-ended, universal program for which every student is eligible for, especially one that is set up to continue in perpetuity or for a very long time, provides the strongest message for families that they should invest in that community.

Community alignment. Promise scholarship programs do not transform communities through funding alone. Rather, community alignment—the degree to which diverse community members buy in to the program and do their part to make it successful—is essential if the transformative potential of Promise programs is to be achieved. A universal program sends the message that the Promise program is not for a select group of students (whether low-income or high-achieving) but rather for the community itself, thus having the potential to elicit a higher level of buy-in and deeper community alignment than a targeted program.

The community transformation goals of the Promise model require a new way of thinking about scholarships—not as limited, competitive opportunities for a given number of qualified students, but as open-ended and inclusive opportunities for students of all types to increase their human capital, and in turn the economic health of their community. Promise programs require broad participation—when more students increase their levels of education, the better it is for the economy—and any additional requirements reduce rather than increase usage. For example, a community service component, while admirable, will increase administrative complexity, complicate evaluation, and make the scholarship unusable for some otherwise qualified students. For stakeholders embracing added requirements as a way of limiting cost, there are far more effective cost-containment strategies than limiting a Promise program to the fulfillment of a series of requirements, well intended or not.

FIT WITH CRITICAL NEED

Regardless of where one stands on the universal versus targeted debate, most people would agree that social programs should be designed to meet the goals of their stakeholders. When staff members from the Upjohn Institute consult with community stakeholders interested in starting Promise programs, we begin by asking a single question: What is your critical need? Designing a Promise program in the absence of a clear answer is a poor idea, since a program's structure should create the incentives necessary to meet this need.

In Hammond, that critical need was increasing the home ownership rate; a program limited to the children of home owners made sense for that community. In Bay County, Michigan, fewer than 18 percent of adults aged 25 and older hold a bachelor's degree; the community foundation created the Bay Commitment Scholarship for first-generation college-going students—a $2,000 award for students from families where the parents do not hold postsecondary degrees.

Sometimes stakeholders have deep beliefs about what is important for success, which may be embedded in the structure of Promise programs even at the expense of greater complexity. In Cleveland County, North Carolina, for example, the Cleveland County Promise is awarded to any student who has an 85 percent high school attendance record and successfully completes an online money management/financial literacy curriculum.

Some Promise programs are linked to a school reform agenda that is committed to raising achievement; the merit terms of the scholarship are used to reinforce efforts by the school district to more adequately prepare students for postsecondary education. If a community's critical need is to raise achievement levels among high school students and create a culture of high expectations throughout the K–12 system, a merit-based program may help with this. But with clear messaging around the value of higher achievement—and the greater monetary value of a scholarship to a more selective institution—universal programs can also accomplish this goal. The strongest argument for universal programs, however, is their power as tools of transformation: in building a college-going culture that is relevant for all students, including those seeking technical training instead of an academic degree, and in inviting community members to buy into the program, thereby leveraging the place-based scholarship into a powerful catalyst for community change.

Notes

1. Hammond's College Bound remains one of only a handful of place-based scholarships funded with public money. The city originally used gaming revenues from the Horseshoe Casino to pay for the program, switching in 2014 to a different source of municipal finance—water service contracts with the state.

2. A complete database of place-based scholarship programs can be found on the Upjohn Institute's website at http://www.upjohn.org/sites/default/files/promise/Lumina/Promisescholarshipprograms.pdf.

3. A third critical question is how much support the scholarship provides. This will depend, in turn, on a host of factors, including scholarship structure (flat grant or variable); what expenses are covered (tuition, fees, living costs); and whether the scholarship is calculated on a first- or last-dollar basis (that is, before or after other forms of financial aid). These choices, and some important unintended consequences that flow from them, are covered in Miller-Adams (2015).

4. The Detroit Scholarship Fund has reported such results. Chuck Wilbur, architect of the Michigan Promise Zones, attributes these impacts to the simplicity of what he calls the "Promise wrapper."

5. This may be starting to change, as at least two planning efforts spearheaded by city governments are considering needs-based scholarships in line with the critical need of combating poverty and increasing social mobility.

6. This rate varies by type of institution, with a six-year graduation rate of 57 percent at public institutions, 66 percent at private nonprofit institutions, and 32 percent at private for-profit institutions.

Chapter 5

Educational Outcomes
of Promise Programs

The Kalamazoo Promise celebrates its tenth anniversary in 2015, yet our knowledge about its impact, and that of the scholarship programs that have followed in its footsteps, is incomplete. There are plenty of reasons why this is so. Many of the expected outcomes of such programs are very long term, and few have been in existence long enough to generate sufficient data for analysis. Even when results can be documented, as was the case with the dramatic increase in degree attainment for Kalamazoo Promise recipients announced in 2015 (Bartik, Hershbein, and Lachowska 2015), the structural diversity described in the previous chapter makes it unwise to generalize about impact across communities. A further challenge is that most Promise initiatives cover entire school districts, making it difficult to conduct randomized controlled experiments or find appropriate comparison groups to carry out rigorous research that gives insight into causation. Data are hard to come by, requiring delicate working relationships with school districts and the preservation of student privacy. And finally, very few Promise programs have allocated funding for research or evaluation, meaning that the task of assessing impact has fallen mainly to researchers with an interest in the topic but limited financial support for their efforts. This poorly resourced, patchwork arrangement contrasts with the federally funded Promise Neighborhoods and Promise Zones efforts, both of which mandate extensive data collection and evaluation and provide the resources with which to conduct them.

The lack of robust research findings also presents a challenge for Promise stakeholders who are replicating the place-based scholarship model without a clear idea of its expected impacts. Critical design choices are being made without a full understanding of their implications or because of cost considerations alone (which can be misunderstood or miscalculated). At the same time, community stakeholders are eager to know what benefits to expect from Promise programs. These factors taken together raise the possibility that new place-based scholarships may overpromise and underdeliver.

Fortunately, despite the methodological challenges noted above, a body of research is beginning to emerge in the bottom-up fashion that seems to characterize the Promise movement overall. In this chapter, I review some of the most interesting findings about the impact of Promise programs to date. Most of this research of necessity focuses on the earliest programs or those where evaluation resources have been available: the Kalamazoo Promise, Pittsburgh Promise, and El Dorado Promise. In surveying the available research, it is also important to note the distinction between data collected and analyzed by school districts or Promise programs themselves and more rigorous research carried out by independent evaluators or academic researchers that seeks to explore causal relationships between a Promise program and student outcomes. Some of this research has been supported with funding from Promise programs; for example, the Pittsburgh Promise has devoted substantial resources to hiring outside evaluators to assess its impact, while in other cases it has been funded by foundation grants or endowments.

In organizing these research findings, I return to the three sets of goals that Promise stakeholders have articulated: 1) transforming K–12 systems through the creation of a college-going culture and incentives for higher achievement, 2) increasing postsecondary access and attainment by reducing financial and nonfinancial barriers to college-going, and 3) stimulating economic revitalization by attracting businesses and residents and/or developing a better-educated workforce.[1] Research findings related to the first two education-related goals are reviewed in this chapter, while the community-level goal is addressed in Chapter 6.

Embedded in the aspirations of Promise stakeholders are implicit goals related to educational inequality. While only a handful of Promise programs target students with financial need, almost all serve school districts that enroll high proportions of low-income and minority students. As a result, such programs have the potential to positively impact students with college-going and completion rates below those of students from more affluent districts. Whether they in fact do so depends on the structure of the Promise program and the range of student support activities it leverages. It is important to ask whether place-based scholarships provide differential benefits to middle- and low-income students, or to white and nonwhite students. Researchers address these questions by routinely segmenting their data by race, ethnicity, and income to determine how outcomes may differ across population groups.

TRANSFORMING K–12 SYSTEMS

A place-based scholarship program can be expected to improve K–12 outcomes by providing incentives for higher achievement in the form of free college tuition and leveraging a system of in- and out-of-school supports to help students better prepare for college access and success. Merit-based programs make these assumptions explicit by providing scholarships only to high school graduates above a certain GPA level and attendance threshold. Universal programs accept as implied the assumption that students will work harder to gain access to scholarships to more selective—and more expensive—institutions.

There are several distinct paths to improved K–12 outcomes. One direct path is that students will strive to improve their effort and attainment because of the incentive provided by the scholarship. Another direct effect of Promise programs is to attract new students into a school district. If the new population is higher achieving than the existing student population, then a district's overall achievement levels will also go up. (To determine which of these dynamics are at work, researchers need student-level data about achievement levels, as well as information about student entry and exit patterns after the announcement of a Promise program.)

The indirect path is equally important. Promise programs by their nature challenge school districts to do better. Especially for universal scholarship programs, teachers must treat every student as "college material," school districts are motivated to innovate around college readiness activities, and students are given an incentive to extend their outlook beyond high school graduation. All these factors create an environment that supports school district improvement, and achievement goes up not just because individual students are working harder but because the entire climate has changed (Miron, Jones, and Young 2009).

These dynamics create additional challenges for researchers who must detect the impact of Promise programs on academic performance without a readily available comparison group and disentangle the direct effects on students from the indirect effects of school climate. Economists have approached this issue in different ways, as the following summaries of three research efforts suggest.

Two of the most rigorous studies to date on the achievement effects of the Kalamazoo Promise come from my colleagues at the Upjohn Institute. The first (Bartik and Lachowska 2012) examines achievement effects in the K–12 setting, and the second (Bartik, Hershbein, and Lachowska 2015, addressed below) looks at college completion data. In a working paper that was subsequently published as a book chapter, Bartik and Lachowska took advantage of the unexpected announcement of the Kalamazoo Promise to study its effects on student achievement and behavior in high school. Comparing the same students before and after the introduction of the Kalamazoo Promise, they examine how the achievement and behavior of individual students eligible for a tuition subsidy differed because of the Promise, compared to what would have occurred without the scholarship program. They find clear evidence that the Kalamazoo Promise reduced student behavior problems and had a dramatic positive effect on high school GPA of African American students. (Estimates of the program's GPA effect for all students were not precise enough to draw strong conclusions.) As the authors note, their study, by its nature, captures only the individual student-level effect of the introduction of the Kalamazoo Promise and thus may understate its impact: "Promise effects that stem from changes in the school district's atmosphere or morale or better peer effects cannot be estimated by our methodology" (Bartik and Lachowska 2012, p. 30).

In a related study of the academic impact of the El Dorado Promise, Ash and Ritter (2014) of the University of Arkansas at Fayetteville examine test scores of El Dorado Public Schools students in grades three through eight. Using student-level achievement and demographic data available for all students across the state of Arkansas, the authors create a hypothetical match for every El Dorado Promise–eligible student. Their research shows that El Dorado Promise students outscored their matched peers by roughly 14 percent of a standard deviation better in math and by 17 percent of a standard deviation in literacy, or the equivalent of six to seven percentile points for students starting near the midpoint of the scoring distribution. Disaggregation by race and income shows test score gains that were especially strong for African American and low-income students in the upper half of the ability distribution—that is, the greatest gains were made by high-achieving students from disadvantaged groups who have strong academic ability but presumably face challenges in attaining postsecondary education.

These two studies reflect improved performance by students in response to the introduction of a Promise program with universal eligibility provisions. A third study, by Doug Harris of Tulane University, addresses a more limited program called The Degree Project. This program is a partnership of Great Lakes Higher Education Corporation and Milwaukee Public Schools that offers merit-based scholarships to one cohort of ninth graders, or approximately 2,600 students, in a randomly selected group of Milwaukee Public Schools high schools. Harris and former colleagues at the University of Wisconsin are investigating the subsequent high school performance and postsecondary attainment of this group of scholarship recipients relative to the population that did not receive the scholarship (Harris 2013). While the research approach may be rigorous, findings from The Degree Project do not represent a true evaluation of the Promise model because scholarships are available to only one cohort of students in selected schools. This means that there is unlikely to be the kind of transformation in overall school culture or peer effects that support improved performance in schools with universal and more far-reaching programs.[2]

A number of studies from disciplines other than economics contribute to a preliminary understanding of what is taking place in K–12 settings in response to Promise programs. Soon after the announcement of the Kalamazoo Promise, faculty and staff at Western Michigan University's Evaluation Center surveyed a variety of populations affected by the Kalamazoo Promise, including students, parents, teachers, and community members. Based on this information, survey respondents reported a number of positive effects on school climate, teacher expectations, and student aspirations (Miron, Jones, and Young 2009). Similarly, researchers from the RAND Corporation identify rising student aspirations as among the early impacts of the Pittsburgh Promise (Gonzalez et al. 2011).

There are a host of indicators that Promise stakeholders can track to assess the impact of their program. Some of these are measures of student achievement that have predictive power for future college success (for example, earning a 3.0 GPA in high school or dual enrollment in a college course), while others are measures that are likely to be affected by the introduction of a Promise program (for example, the prevalence of advanced placement).

Of special interest are graduation and dropout rates, since students cannot take advantage of a college scholarship program if they do not receive a high school diploma (GED recipients are generally ineligible for Promise scholarships). The expectation is that the availability of free college tuition will create an incentive for students to stay in school until graduation. But significant improvements in high school graduation rates have been slow to materialize, and even understanding the trends is problematic. Consider the case of Kalamazoo. High school graduation and dropout rates are notoriously difficult to track because when a student leaves a school system it is not always clear if he or she has dropped out or simply relocated to another district. In 2007, the state of Michigan began tracking graduation and dropout rates in a new and more sophisticated way that captures in-state transfers among districts; however, these data are not available for the pre-Promise period, so pre- and post–Kalamazoo Promise comparisons are not possible. Another challenge is that Michigan has changed the high school graduation requirements several times in recent years, generally making them more rigorous and hence more difficult for students to graduate. Finally, if the composition of a school district changes over time, then this will make it less useful to compare graduation rates; for example, an improvement in graduation rates might be the result of improved student effort, or it might reflect a change in the makeup of the student body.

Still, there are some signs that Promise programs are having a positive impact on graduation rates. In Pittsburgh, the graduation rate rose from 65 percent in 2009 to 71 percent for the class of 2014. Denver Public Schools reports historically high increases in graduation rates between 2007 and 2013, with the district halving the gap between its graduation rate and the state average (Denver Public Schools 2014). In Kalamazoo, graduation rates are slowly trending upward (from 64 percent in 2009 to 69 percent in 2014).[3] One interesting feature is that five-year cohort graduation rates have been consistently higher than four-year rates, suggesting that some students may be opting to stay in school an extra year (or even just for the summer) to complete the credits necessary to get a high school diploma. Here, too, segmenting of data is essential. In Kalamazoo, for example, four-year graduation rates are rising for every demographic group, with African American females graduating at rates that exceed the state average. Low-income students and African American males lag other demographic groups in their graduation rates (Mack 2015b).

Data issues notwithstanding, there are at least two powerful reasons Promise programs may not have the impact on high school graduation rates that stakeholders have hoped for. Promise programs, especially those that are merit based, simply may not hold much attraction for struggling students, who are at the highest risk for dropping out. For someone who dislikes school, the lure of a college scholarship that provides money for more schooling is not very strong. One solution is to ensure that career planning begins in middle school and that students understand the range of career and technical programs that are covered by Promise scholarships. Pittsburgh's experiment that allows students to use Promise funding for vocational training while still in high school may provide a model for other communities grappling with this issue.

A second reason the impact of Promise programs on graduation rates may be limited concerns the achievement gap. It is unlikely that a student starting high school with low academic skills—a common scenario in an urban district—will make up enough ground to graduate in four years, let alone meet the requirements needed for a merit scholarship. For students at the margin, the option for a fifth year or personal curriculum tailored to one's individual abilities may be useful. Early commitment scholarship programs also help by providing strong academic and behavioral support throughout middle and high school. But strategies for closing achievement gaps in K–12 education must reach much further down the developmental continuum, to early childhood interventions, high-quality pre-K, and support for struggling families, underscoring the need for Promise programs to be part of a broader community-based strategy.

For those students who do graduate from high school, the issue of college readiness is important to Promise stakeholders and researchers. The impact of Promise programs on postsecondary outcomes is addressed in the following section, but here it is useful to note that school districts have responded to Promise programs by ramping up their college readiness activities. Some data are available to suggest that these efforts are paying off. In Denver, a large part of Denver

Scholarship Foundation funding has gone to support the creation of Future Centers in 12 high schools that serve students at 21 schools. Each center is staffed by a full-time college advisor who guides students through the college application and financial aid processes.

A number of other communities, including La Crosse, Wisconsin, and Lynchburg, Virginia, have incorporated the Future Centers model into their Promise programs. Other communities, including El Dorado and Kalamazoo, have focused on the expansion of advanced placement (AP) classes as a proxy for college readiness, encouraging more students to attempt AP credits and expanding the availability of course selection. Historically, economically disadvantaged and minority students have been the least likely to avail themselves of AP offerings.

In El Dorado, AP course offerings have been expanded, and the number of students taking AP tests more than doubled between 2005 and 2013 (El Dorado Promise 2015). In Kalamazoo, counselors now enroll any promising student in AP courses, and AP enrollment of disadvantaged groups has mushroomed. From 2007–2008 to 2014–2015, the number of students taking AP courses more than doubled, while the number of AP courses these students took more than tripled. Over this period, the number of low-income students taking AP courses rose from 63 to 263, the number of African American students rose from 53 to 193, and the number of Hispanic students rose from 8 to 78 (Mack 2014).

Perhaps not surprisingly, the pass rate for AP exams (the fee for which is now covered by the district for all students enrolled in AP courses) has gone down, although the number of students passing with a score of three or higher (often sufficient to gain college credit) has gone up, from 143 to 380. Some parents have expressed concern that the AP curriculum has been watered down and that AP classes are now subject to the kinds of behavioral disruptions that are common in traditional courses. There are other concerns that pushing academically unprepared students to take AP classes may further discourage students who are already struggling. On balance, though, the exposure to an AP curriculum and experience of taking the AP test is valuable preparation for college, giving students without any "college knowledge" a better sense of what it will take to be successful in a postsecondary setting.

POSTSECONDARY OUTCOMES

Reducing the barriers to college access, especially for first-generation and low-income potential college-goers, is one of the central goals of virtually every place-based scholarship program. College success, as measured by retention and degree or certificate completion, is just as important as access. What do we know thus far about the postsecondary outcomes of Promise programs?

To begin with, we know more about postsecondary *access* than we do about degree *completion*, and the case of the Kalamazoo Promise provides a good explanation of why. The first meaningful trend data about changes in college completion due to the Kalamazoo Promise did not become available until 2014, a full eight years after the first class of Promise-eligible students went to college. The reason is that college completion rates at four-year institutions are generally tracked over a six-year time frame; the first college completion data for the class of 2006 thus did not become available until 2012, and not until three years of data were available (2012, 2013, and 2014) did my economist colleagues at the Upjohn Institute see the improvement in degree completion that many observers expected would be one of the results of the program.

In their 2015 paper, "Effects of the Kalamazoo Promise Scholarship on College Enrollment, Persistence, and Completion," Timothy Bartik, Brad Hershbein, and Marta Lachowska find a large increase in college enrollment concentrated at four-year institutions and a moderate increase in credits attempted in the first two, three, and four years after high school graduation. The biggest news from their study is a dramatic gain of 25 percent in credential attainment within six years of high school graduation, with an even larger percentage increase of 33 percent if only bachelor's degrees are considered. The magnitude of the boost to credential attainment is not significantly different with income or race; however, the estimates suggest that credential effects for women are greater than for men.

Another expected impact of Promise programs, especially those like the Kalamazoo Promise that effectively reduce the cost of tuition (although not the total cost of college) to zero, is a shift in the post-secondary institutions students choose to attend. While the high and rising cost of tuition is not the only barrier to postsecondary atten-dance, it is an important one. In Promise communities, the reduction in tuition costs can lead to several different types of shifts. Successful students who might have previously attended a low-cost community college before transferring to a more expensive four-year institution may now go directly to those four-year schools. Students who may have opted to live at home to afford the cost of university tuition may now have the freedom to live on campus in a different community. And less academically successful students who may never have con-sidered any kind of postsecondary program now may take advantage of free tuition to give college a try.

At the upper end of the achievement scale, my colleague Bridget Timmeney and I examine college attendance patterns for students graduating from the region's selective math and science center (Miller-Adams and Timmeney 2013). Comparing pre– and post–Kalamazoo Promise data for Promise-eligible and -ineligible groups (from districts other than KPS), we find a dramatic (albeit expected) shift in the direction of the in-state public universities where Promise-eligible students could use their scholarships. This shift came at the expense of both private institutions and out-of-state schools, although the pattern may not hold up in the future now that 15 private Michi-gan colleges are included among Kalamazoo Promise–eligible insti-tutions. It can be argued that the limits imposed by the Kalamazoo Promise may have led students in some cases to choose less selective institutions than they might have otherwise; on the other hand, the extent of the shift suggests the strong attraction of earning a bachelor's degree without accumulating a high debt load, especially for a group of students who are likely to go on to graduate study.

Data from the Kalamazoo Promise reveal a key finding about college success for scholarship recipients: there is a marked divergence in success measures between those students who can gain admission to four-year institutions and those who cannot. The first group is progressing and graduating at the same rate as the general population of those institutions, while the second—those with lower GPAs who for the most part are attending two-year community colleges—is struggling, as are their peers at those institutions. And because more low-income students and students of color lag in K–12 achievement, they are more likely to be in that second group. As a result, retention and completion show a significant divide along racial lines, with students of color half as likely to complete as white students.

Persistent disparities in progression and completion along racial and socioeconomic lines will not be addressed by scholarship dollars alone. One of the challenges of universal eligibility programs is that some of the students making use of the scholarship will be underprepared for college in terms of both hard and soft skills. Experience from Kalamazoo and other communities, however, suggests that the innovation and close partnerships that Promise programs often leverage can serve to reduce these gaps, as the following example suggests.

Over half of all Kalamazoo Promise students at some point take classes at Kalamazoo Valley Community College (KVCC), the local two-year institution. In response, KVCC created a Student Success Center in 2007 that serves all students with individualized support around academic, personal, and career needs. The Kalamazoo Promise modified its program rules early on to allow students to attend KVCC part time, in recognition of the reality that many students at two-year institutions often have work and family obligations. KVCC and the Promise staff use data to evaluate the performance of Promise students enrolled there and to inform them about program changes and improvements. Mandatory support services for Promise students who are new to the institution or are academically underperforming are currently being introduced. The results have been a significant improvement in academic performance for Promise students attending KVCC. Improvements include higher GPAs, more classes successfully completed, and better performance in developmental courses. More specifically,

- the average GPA for Promise students during their first semester at KVCC has risen from 1.5 to 2.0;

- the average GPA for all Promise students at KVCC has risen from 1.5 to 2.2;

- the percentage of classes completed with at least a 2.0 grade has increased from less than 45 percent to nearly 65 percent; and

- there has been a 50 percent reduction in classes for which students earned no credits; in other words, the frequency with which students drop or fail a class has been reduced by half.[4]

When it comes to assessing postsecondary outcomes, a different analytic strategy is needed for merit-based programs such as the Pittsburgh Promise. In addition, results from these programs will not be strictly comparable to those from universal programs, because the student populations will necessarily be different. Place-based scholarships with merit floors go to students who, by definition, are relatively well prepared for college success. In a study of postsecondary retention and persistence by Pittsburgh Promise scholars, researchers at the University of Pittsburgh found that Promise scholars were retained at higher rates (from year one to year two of college) than the national average at virtually every type of postsecondary institution (Iriti, Bickel, and Kaufman 2012). Performance was especially strong at two-year institutions, an unsurprising finding since students eligible for the Pittsburgh Promise have a GPA floor of no lower than 2.0, which is higher than that of many students at open-admission institutions. As the researchers put it, "some of the Promise advantage in these [institutions] could be explained by the Promise GPA criterion."

Iriti, Bickel, and Kaufman also examine the related phenomenon of persistence, or whether students are on track to complete a credential or degree. In examining the factors responsible for persistence, they find that being female, having a higher income, having a higher GPA, and attending a more selective institution are predictive of higher rates of persistence.

Additional research on postsecondary outcomes will become available in 2016, as a Lumina Foundation–funded research project comes to a close. This project, initiated in 2014, represents aligned research into postsecondary outcomes by scholars in five communities—Buffalo, El Dorado, Kalamazoo, New Haven, and Pittsburgh—as well as some cross-site analyses of additional programs. The preliminary findings of the researchers will be presented at PromiseNet 2015, and final papers and research findings will be available on both the PromiseNet website and the W.E. Upjohn Institute website.

The third set of Promise goals, variously framed as economic development, workforce development, community transformation, or improved quality of life, are addressed in the next chapter. For the most part, these community-level effects are qualitatively different from both K–12 and postsecondary outcomes in that they are harder to measure, there are fewer ready sources of data, and it is more difficult to determine causality. (One exception is enrollment effects for local school districts where some dramatic changes have occurred.) Chapter 6 turns to the pressing question of whether Promise programs can indeed serve to promote economic development or community transformation, as so many of their stakeholders hope.

Notes

1. These goals were identified in an unpublished survey of the websites and founding documents of Promise programs carried out by W.E. Upjohn Institute researchers in 2011.
2. In August 2015, it was announced that 418 graduates had qualified for a scholarship from The Degree Project and would receive $5 million in funding. This means that of the 2,600 students in the initial ninth grade

cohort, only 16 percent ultimately received scholarships, underscoring the selective nature of merit-based programs with strict criteria (Great Lakes Higher Education Corporation 2015).
3. These percentages are not comparable across the different communities, as various states calculate graduation rates using different methodologies. In all cases, however, the increases in graduation rates are especially meaningful because methods are generally changing in ways that would depress graduation rates and, in some states (including Michigan), graduation requirements, too, have been tightened.
4. Kalamazoo Promise data.

Chapter 6

The Elusive Economic Development Goal

Perhaps the most important difference between traditional scholarships and Promise programs is the latter's emphasis on community transformation. Almost every place-based scholarship program includes goals that encompass nonacademic, or community-level effects. The Pittsburgh Promise seeks to "deploy a well-prepared and energized workforce."[1] The El Dorado Promise counts a "vibrant economy" and "improved quality of life" among its expected achievements.[2] The New Haven Promise refers to a desire to "enhance growth, stability, and economic development of the city of New Haven."[3] Economic development, a better quality of life, and a well-trained workforce are various expressions of the hoped-for community-level outcomes of place-based scholarship programs.

The empirical case for expecting these results from a place-based scholarship is hard to make. Instead, these expectations rest both on intuition about what makes a community more desirable and on scholarly findings about the relationship between educational levels and a community's economic health. Before turning to this relationship, it bears considering why it is so difficult to directly demonstrate the economic development impact of Promise programs. There are at least three challenges.

The first is that the time frame over which economic development activities unfold can be quite long. While the announcement of a place-based scholarship program may provide an immediate boost to family finances, student effort, and school climate, the decisions by individuals and businesses that could contribute to an improving economy take longer to make. Even 10 years on, the direct economic impact of the Kalamazoo Promise has been modest, amounting to additional financial resources flowing to the school district because of rising enrollment, new school construction, and the use of a large proportion of scholarship funding at local institutions. More profound economic impacts, such as rising levels of education in the workforce, population growth, or higher family incomes, may take decades to become evident. In this sense, it is too early to judge the economic development impact of even the earliest Promise programs, and even more premature to evaluate the impact of other, newer programs.

A second challenge relates to the difficulty of drawing conclusions about causality when it comes to nonschool effects. As one moves away from the direct beneficiaries of Promise scholarships—students, families, and schools—to the broader community, it becomes harder to identify the scholarship program as a causal factor in positive developments under way. Whether one is examining the housing market, business creation, downtown development, or population shifts, multiple causes are at work. The intervention of a place-based scholarship program, even one as generous and open ended as the Kalamazoo Promise, can easily be overshadowed by larger trends, such as changes in the housing market, economic conditions, or the culmination of decades of efforts by local economic development entities. While there may be little doubt in the minds of residents that a scholarship program is having a positive impact on the local economy, it is virtually impossible to document a clear causal relationship between a scholarship program and economic development outcomes.

A third and related challenge is what social scientists call the problem of the counterfactual. There is no way to know how local economic development might have evolved in the absence of a place-based scholarship program. In Kalamazoo, one can surmise that the local economy would have continued on much the same path, with weakness in the housing market, downtown development efforts struggling to maintain momentum, and the urban core continuing to lose residents. But it is difficult to know how pronounced these trends might have been and whether other factors could have come along to reverse them. In the absence of this counterfactual and given the other methodological constraints mentioned above, the best that researchers can do is draw reasonable conclusions from available data while sounding a cautionary note that although place-based scholarship programs can contribute to economic development, they are not a quick fix for communities in decline.

Setting these challenges aside, what is the case for investing in education as a path to economic development? Two strands of academic literature offer some answers to this question. The first concerns the linkages among educational levels, productivity, and economic growth, while the second addresses the role of a strong central city in regional vitality.

EDUCATION AND ECONOMIC GROWTH

Extensive research correlates higher education and skill levels with greater productivity, and greater productivity with faster rates of economic growth. Not surprisingly, as an individual increases his or her human capital—defined as the skills that people are endowed with or acquire through investment in training and education—the more productive he or she will be as a worker. This is what underpins the wider range of job choice, higher earnings potential, and lower unemployment rates for skilled or educated workers. Research also shows that the benefits of more education accrue not only to the individual but also to the community in which he or she lives. Businesses maximize productivity in part by gaining access to a well-trained and productive workforce; as a result, cities and regions rich in workers with high human capital are among the most attractive places for businesses to locate.

In exploring the connection between human capital and regional growth, economists Edward L. Glaeser of Harvard University and Albert Saiz of MIT find that, apart from climate and immigration patterns, "skill composition may be the most powerful predictor of urban growth. This is both a boon to the skilled cities that have done spectacularly over the past two decades and a curse to the cities with less skilled workers that have suffered an almost unstoppable urban decline" (Glaeser and Saiz 2003, p. 42). Glaeser and Saiz argue that human capital matters most in potentially declining places. Skills are especially valuable in these settings because they help cities adapt and change in response to negative economic shocks. This finding has clear implications for urban policy: "City growth can be promoted with strategies that increase the level of local human capital" (p. 43), including the provision of quality public schools. A high-quality educational system plays two roles, attracting educated workers to a community while producing more of them through graduation and access to higher education.

Promise programs offer a good example of this dual dynamic. The availability of scholarships creates an incentive for workers and businesses who value education to move to or remain within the community. At the same time, such programs increase incentives for local school districts to educate and graduate students who are prepared to pursue some kind of postsecondary education. Over time, these two paths should converge to yield a more skilled local workforce.

Elaborating on the education-economy connection, Glaeser and Berry (2006) have shown that regions with skilled workforces ("smart regions") experience higher rates of population and income growth than those without these assets. Their research finds that regions where more than 25 percent of the population had college degrees in 1980 saw their population surge by 45 percent on average over the subsequent 20 years, while low-skilled metropolitan areas (those where fewer than 10 percent of adults had college degrees in 1980) grew on average by just 13 percent. In addition, even unskilled workers located in the smart cities earned significantly more than their counterparts in metropolitan areas with lower levels of educational attainment (of course, the cost of living is also usually higher in these areas). Human capital investment strategies are increasingly important in part because the gap in educational attainment between skilled and less-skilled areas has accelerated. One possible reason is that entrepreneurs in the past tended to hire large numbers of unskilled workers, whereas today's most successful businesses rely on highly educated workers. In a virtuous circle in which smart places are getting smarter, regions with an initial advantage in human capital are better able to attract employers who provide jobs for workers with high levels of skills and education.

Why might a local skills-based economic development strategy be more important today, compared to the past? As has been noted by many, skills are more crucial to the U.S. economy and competitiveness today because of technological change and growing global competition. Furthermore, businesses are more footloose today than in the past and are less tied in location decisions to natural resources or markets. Although it might seem strange, one of the least mobile resources today is the local labor force, making it more of a strategic factor for communities seeking an economic comparative advantage. Finally, with increased income inequality in the United States, it is more important than ever to identify economic development strategies that can share the benefits of development more broadly with the local population, which an emphasis on skills of local residents can accomplish.

Place-based scholarship programs make it possible for a large proportion of the community's youth to obtain new skills and increase the likelihood of educated workers being attracted to a community. As a result, the communities that are home to such programs can expect higher rates of income growth for all residents.

STRENGTHENING THE URBAN CORE

The education-productivity-income link described above generally applies throughout a metropolitan region; however, the Kalamazoo Promise and most programs like it are targeted toward high-poverty school districts that serve a region's urban core. Why does it make economic sense to invest in urban schools? Beyond concerns about equality of opportunity, this choice may reflect a growing understanding that a region is only as strong as its core. "Regional economies are integrated wholes, with different parts of the metropolitan area specializing in different economic functions," write Dreier, Mollenkopf, and Swanstrom (2001, p. 25). "[O]lder central cities continue to provide large pools of private assets, accumulated knowledge, sophisticated skills, cultural resources, and social networks." Glaeser, in his book *Triumph of the City* (2011), makes another case for the value of having a strong urban center, showing how cities attract talent, make possible the face-to-face interaction that spurs innovation, and create avenues for social and economic mobility.

While a few cities have bucked the trend, most of the nation's urban areas have lost population, wealth, and influence since the 1970s. This is especially true for those older cities located in the Northeast and upper Midwest that had been at the heart of the nation's manufacturing economy for much of the twentieth century. In an account of one of the more extreme examples of these trends, historian and sociologist Thomas J. Sugrue identifies three forces that accounted for the urban crisis in Detroit (and, by extension, other metropolitan areas): the flight of jobs, especially the unionized manufacturing jobs that characterized the post–World War II urban economy, the persistence of workplace discrimination, and racial segregation in housing that led to an uneven distribution of power and resources in metropolitan areas (Sugrue 1996). We could add to this list poor civic leadership, institutional sclerosis, and a decline in federal support for programs that aid cities.

Such deep structural trends may be impossible to reverse, but a long-term human capital investment strategy, such as that offered by Promise programs, is one path for the revitalization of these urban areas. Bruce Katz, codirector of the Metropolitan Policy Program of the Brookings Institution, has written extensively about the advantages of a dense and vibrant urban core, and he and his colleagues have proposed a set of federal urban policy initiatives to support an uneven, but potentially important, resurgence of population under way in some cities. "The key to growing an urban middle class is simple: education. With residential choice dependent on school quality, cities need to ensure that their schools can attract and retain families with broader options" (Katz 2006, p. 15). What about the poor? Many scholars, Sugrue among them, have noted that urban revitalization often fails to benefit the low-income individuals who live in the central city: "There has been very little 'trickle down' from downtown revitalization and neighborhood gentrification to the long-term poor, the urban working class, and minorities. An influx of coffee shops, bistros, art galleries, and upscale boutiques have made parts of many cities increasingly appealing for the privileged, but they have not, in any significant way, altered the everyday misery and impoverishment that characterize many urban neighborhoods" (Sugrue 1996, p. xxv). Education, especially education for the children of the urban working class and poor, might resolve this tension, bringing benefits to those who need them most.

Economic consultant Jeff Thredgold, writing shortly after the Kalamazoo Promise was announced, recognized the potential importance of a human capital–centered strategy for a declining urban community:

> Communities facing hard times have traditionally focused on such things as new public buildings, business parks, and the like as a means of enticing new employers and new residents to a community. Temporary tax breaks and incentives have also been tried frequently. Success has been limited. The Promise is different. The enticement of new residents to the community to take advantage of funding of their children's college educations is a strong one. Given tight labor markets across the nation, new companies are also likely to consider Kalamazoo as a place to do business as they see a rising population. The lure of more and more college graduates in the local labor force in coming years is also a powerful incentive to locate a business in Kalamazoo. (Thredgold 2007, p. 2)

By situating education at the center of the community's economic development strategy, Promise programs emphasize the importance of human capital to a city's future and provide incentives for its creation. Different types of Promise programs accomplish this in different ways—restrictive scholarships focused on the local community college may have a more direct contribution to workforce development, while expansive programs with four-year options will be more effective in attracting middle-class families into a community.

ECONOMIC DEVELOPMENT IMPACT

Is there any evidence that Promise programs are bringing measurable economic benefits to the communities in which they are located? In this section, I review the main economic effects of the Kalamazoo Promise on the local school district, students and families, and the city and region, while referencing research findings from other Promise communities.

In most Promise communities, the school district is one of the earliest and most visible beneficiaries of a place-based scholarship program. This has certainly been the case in Kalamazoo, where enrollment in the KPS district rose by 24 percent in the nine years following the introduction of the Promise. The enrollment increase marked a reversal of several decades of decline (see Figure 6.1) and has brought the district many benefits, including additional dollars (since state funding for schools is based on the number of students they enroll), voter support for large bond issues that have made possible the construction of new schools (the first new buildings in the district in almost 40 years) and the renovation of other facilities, and improved public perceptions of the school district (Miller-Adams and Fiore 2013).

In a series of papers, my colleagues at the Upjohn Institute have examined the nature of this enrollment increase. In their 2010 analysis, Tim Bartik, Randy Eberts, and Wei-Jang Huang find that increased

Figure 6.1 Kalamazoo Public Schools' Long-Term Enrollment Trend

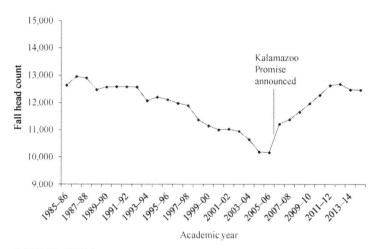

SOURCE: KPS data.

school district enrollment following the introduction of the Promise was due both to increased student entry into the district and a marked decline in exit rates. While the initial post-Promise enrollment boost was about equally due to an increase in entrants and a decline in exit rates, the subsequent enrollment increase is almost entirely due to a reduction in exit rates. This suggests that the Promise has served to attach families to the district for a longer period, which was clearly one of the donors' goals, given the sliding scale of benefits.

Increased enrollment has had important effects on school finances and local economic development. Bartik, Eberts, and Huang (2010) calculate that without the Promise, KPS enrollments would have declined by almost 500 students between 2005 and 2009. Instead of the projected 9,701 students the district would have enrolled without the Promise, by fall 2009, the student count was 12,106, or a difference of about 25 percent. (Enrollment has continued to increase since 2009, although at a slower pace than the initial boost.) These additional students represented an $18.7 million state funding boost to the KPS budget in 2009–2010. And because the marginal cost of serving a new student is below the value of the additional state funding received per pupil, the authors calculate that the district had an additional $6 million to spend on new services for students.

The authors also find that the Promise stabilized the demographic balance in the district, following decades of white flight. Enrollment increases were seen in the white, black, and Hispanic population, roughly in proportion to each group's initial enrollment. Table 6.1 shows the percentage of different racial and ethnic groups pre- and post-Promise. The 2005 and 2009 data are comparable, but by 2014, KPS had added a multiracial category that explains some of the decline in African American enrollments. Notably, in contrast to some expectations, the Promise has not served to draw large numbers of middle-class students; in fact, the percentage of students qualifying for free and reduced meals has actually increased (although this is likely due in part to the tough economic climate of the past decade).

Stabilization of the racial, ethnic, and socioeconomic composition of the district is important for several reasons. First, it may be a valuable social goal in and of itself (and there is extensive research supporting the benefits of socioeconomic school integration for the learning of all students; see, for example, Kahlenberg [2012]). Second, a racially and economically integrated school district may be better able to maintain political (and financial) support from a diverse community and is more likely to be attractive to potential migrants to Kalamazoo. Thus, the stabilization of school demographics in Kalamazoo (which becomes even more apparent when one compares it to neighboring urban school districts) may have important implications for the community's future economic vitality.

In a subsequent paper, Hershbein (2013) takes a second look at the enrollment boost that followed the Kalamazoo Promise, analyzing the origins and destinations, socioeconomic composition, and individual school choices associated with the inflow of students. Results show that the majority of students who entered KPS the year after the Promise was announced came from outside district boundaries, and a quarter of new students came from out of state, suggesting the migra-

**Table 6.1 Kalamazoo Public Schools Demographic (population group
as percentage of student body)**

	2005	2009	2014
African American	48.2	47.5	41.0
Hispanic	8.5	10.1	9.8
White	40.2	39.3	37.6
Multiracial[a]	n/a	n/a	9.3
Low-income (of all races)	62	69	69

[a]The multiracial category was not available in 2005 or 2009.
SOURCE: KPS data.

tion of new households into the area. Over half of new students came
from other Michigan school districts, most from within Kalamazoo
County. Conversely, the proportion of students that exited KPS who
did so to attend neighboring districts fell from 80 percent to 50 percent
in the years following the announcement of the Promise. The findings
suggest considerable economic benefits not just for the school district
but for the broader metropolitan area.

Few other Promise communities have seen enrollment increases
comparable to what has unfolded in Kalamazoo, although there is
some evidence of positive enrollment impacts in other locales. For
example, Ash and Ritter (2014) report that prior to the announcement of the El Dorado Promise, the local school district had experienced a decline of nearly 14 percent in overall enrollment from 1990
through 2006. Since the year the Promise was announced, the decline
has halted, and there have been small increases in enrollment. Moreover, the proportion of low-income students enrolled in the El Dorado
schools has held steady while it has increased in comparable districts.
They speculate that this may be due to increased economic vitality
in El Dorado, greater desire by middle-class residents to remain in
the community, or an influx of new middle-class families, concluding
that it is some combination of these factors that has contributed to the
relative economic stability of El Dorado.

Increasing enrollment is also one of the goals of the Pittsburgh Promise, which was designed in part to "mitigate and reverse the population declines in the city of Pittsburgh and the enrollment declines in Pittsburgh public schools."[4] RAND's 2011 study of the Pittsburgh Promise (Gonzalez et al. 2011) and more recent work by consultants from McKinsey & Company have found that, while the district continues to lose students, the rate of loss has slowed significantly.

One of the questions addressed by LeGower and Walsh (2014) in their analysis of the enrollment and housing effects of multiple Promise programs is whether merit-based programs might have different enrollment effects than universal programs. The authors find that public school enrollments increased in Promise communities relative to their surrounding areas following the announcement of a place-based scholarship program; however, they also find distributional effects of interest to those concerned with racial and economic diversity. Programs with the greatest choice of postsecondary institutions experienced the largest enrollment effects, and impacts were highest in the elementary grades (reflecting the sliding scale with greater benefits for long-term enrollment in place in most Promise programs). Schools associated with merit-based programs experienced increases in white enrollment and decreases in nonwhite enrollment. LeGower and Walsh's housing price findings, addressed below, also suggest that universal and merit-based programs have different impacts on the surrounding community.

Beyond school districts, the other immediate beneficiaries of Promise scholarships are the students who make use of them. For families with children eligible for scholarships, among the likely impacts are freed-up college savings, increased disposable income, and a reduced student debt load. The evidence on this front is anecdotal rather than systematic, but stories from Kalamazoo suggest some impact on entrepreneurship as well, with people willing to invest in businesses knowing that their children's college costs are covered.

One economic impact that is well documented is a strong pattern of scholarship use at Kalamazoo's two local postsecondary institutions. Since 2006, nearly two-thirds of Kalamazoo Promise recipients have chosen to attend either the two-year community college or four-year research university located in Kalamazoo. This means not only that the scholarship dollars awarded by the Kalamazoo Promise have gone to local institutions, with Western Michigan University receiving by far the highest payments, but also that student spending has remained within the local economy. With 58 postsecondary institutions to choose from, the dominance of the two local institutions in the college-going patterns of Promise scholars has served as an important economic benefit for the Kalamazoo community.

One of the expected effects of Promise programs is an increase in housing prices. LeGower and Walsh (2014) find that within three years of the announcement of a Promise program, residential properties within selected Promise communities experienced a 7–12 percent increase on average in housing prices relative to the region immediately surrounding the Promise area. They find that housing price effects are larger in neighborhoods with high-quality schools and in the upper half of the housing price distribution, suggesting higher valuation by high-income households. These findings led the authors to conclude that Promise scholarships mainly affect the behavior of households above the median income for which they present the greatest value. Their research also shows that merit-based versions of Promise programs disproportionately affected housing market decisions of white households.

Economic trends in El Dorado since the Promise was announced illustrate the challenges noted at the beginning of this chapter regarding causality. El Dorado has undoubtedly experienced positive economic developments that were immediately preceded by the implementation of the El Dorado Promise. Shortly after the announcement of the program, voters in El Dorado approved a $0.01 sales tax estimated to generate $32 million over eight years, to implement El Dorado Forward, the city's strategic economic development plan. That same year, voters approved a 4.6 mill property tax millage to build a new high school. Excitement over the El Dorado Promise almost certainly played a role in voter support for these two tax requests; however, it is impossible to disentangle the Promise as a cause from other factors that may have influenced the vote. In June 2015, voters by a 2-1 margin approved a renewal of the sales tax, with the Promise playing less of a role in the debate this time.

The El Dorado Promise has contributed to a higher national profile for the community; speakers at its annual signing days have included Presidents George W. Bush and Bill Clinton, and the program has been featured in *People* magazine, the in-flight magazine of American Airlines, and many other venues. El Dorado's downtown was recognized in 2009 by the National Trust for Historic Preservation, and the city has earned multiple City of Distinctions awards.[5] The town's main street is almost fully occupied, and a $70 million arts district renovation is under way, representing one of the largest historic preservation efforts in Arkansas. While these are all positive developments that have coincided with the implementation of the El Dorado Promise, it is impossible to know whether it is the Promise, the strategic plan, or the synergy of the two that has made the difference.

Several other communities have structured their place-based scholarship programs in such a way as to create specific economic development effects. A leader in this area is Hammond, Indiana, which created the College Bound scholarship in 2006 specifically for the children of Hammond home owners. Since 2006, College Bound has awarded over 1,000 last-dollar scholarships of up to $10,500. The local board of realtors and city leaders believe that the program has helped stabilize the city's population despite a forecasted decline, and that, at least until the 2008 financial crisis, College Bound was correlated with higher home sales and reduced time-on-market for single family homes. A recent survey of students who had graduated from the program shows that a sizable proportion had opted to return to Hammond. Program organizers also note that a community service requirement of 40 hours per student has contributed to the city's quality of life, generating 15,800 hours of community service in 2013 alone (College Bound 2013; *Times of Northwest Indiana* 2014).

Stakeholders in La Crosse, Wisconsin, who spent several years evaluating program design options for its Promise program, have opted for a two-part strategy: 1) the creation of Future Centers in the high schools to promote college-going and assist students in accessing scholarships, and 2) a place-based scholarship (not yet operating) that will initially be limited to families who renovate or build homes within the city of La Crosse. The home-building strategy is explicitly targeted at the middle class—homes must have a value of at least $150,000 (above the city's current median of $127,000). The program is designed to increase the density of the urban core, reduce suburban sprawl, and attract middle-class families to the city.

This discussion of economic development strategies highlights an important tension for Promise programs: whether the primary goal should be to support and broaden college access for disadvantaged groups or whether the scholarships should be designed as an incentive to attract more affluent families into a community. Kalamazoo's universal, generous, flexible model has a good chance of accomplishing both goals, while La Crosse is using its Future Centers to serve existing students and its scholarship to attract new middle-class residents.

A second economic development issue worth flagging is the question of whether the school district served by the Promise program is expanding by retaining families and drawing new families from outside the area, or whether it is simply redistributing the existing student population from neighboring school districts, thus having little impact on the broader economy. Research into the enrollment effects of the Kalamazoo Promise suggests a mixed record—many of the new entrants into the district did indeed come from a neighboring school district, almost certainly exacerbating that district's struggle with declining enrollment. Other surrounding districts have held their own, and there is evidence that much of the growth in KPS enrollment has been accomplished through declining exit rates and the attraction of some new students from out of area. This is an economically healthy way to grow a district, organically and from within, through the creation of long-term attachment of families to a single district (and city) thanks to the incentive provided by a place-based scholarship.

In the next chapter I address whether this model is sustainable and identify some of the most important lessons of the Promise movement's first decade.

Notes

1. See the Pittsburgh Promise website: http://www.pittsburghpromise.org/ (accessed July 30, 2015).
2. See the El Dorado Promise website: http://www.eldoradopromise.com (accessed July 30, 2015).
3. See the New Haven Promise website: http://www.newhavenpromise .org/ (accessed July 30, 2015).
4. See Note 1.
5. See http://www.preservationnation.org/main-street/main-street-news/ 2009/02/el-dorado.html (accessed July 29, 2015).

Chapter 7

The Future of the Promise Movement

$\mathbf{P}$romise programs have emerged against the backdrop of three trends: 1) a steep increase in college costs, 2) rising returns to workers with postsecondary degrees or credentials, and 3) urban revitalization strategies that focus on human capital as a path to remaining economically competitive. Place-based scholarships represent a grassroots response to these trends, as communities seek to increase their attractiveness to businesses and residents by reducing the cost of education for a large proportion of their young people. The record of the past 10 years suggests that the model has staying power; it has proven attractive to stakeholders in diverse settings, and the process of replication and innovation continues. But two sets of challenges could slow the enthusiasm that currently characterizes the Promise movement.

First, policy developments could make some Promise programs obsolete. There is little doubt that education will continue to yield high returns to workers and the communities in which they choose to reside. However, changes in college affordability and financial aid could diminish the need for place-based scholarships, especially those that focus on two-year institutions.

Second, it is not clear that the momentum behind Promise programs can be sustained in the absence of demonstrated positive impact on communities. Some Promise programs have already had to scale back their scholarships in light of fund development challenges. And even in places where ample funding is available, money alone does not guarantee results. Will the Promise movement survive if it fails to fulfill its ambitious agenda of school and community change?

This chapter addresses these questions and draws on the decade-long history of the Promise movement to distill some ideas for maximizing impact and sustainability.

THE CHANGING FINANCIAL AID LANDSCAPE

The rising cost of college in recent years has received growing attention from policymakers, the media, and the public. Among the responses are a plethora of state and national initiatives, including FAFSA simplification, college scorecards created by the U.S. Department of Education, and actions by state legislatures to hold tuition increases in check. Some of these efforts seek to increase the availability of financial aid, while others promote transparency and accountability around the costs and benefits of college.

Another response can be found in movements at the local, state, and national levels to make community college free. Many of the place-based scholarships that are the focus of this book provide tuition-free community college to all graduates of a local school district. Tennessee and Oregon will be pioneering this approach at the state level, providing tuition-free community college for all state residents. And President Obama has elevated the issue to the national stage by proposing legislation that would make two years of community college free for individuals in states that choose to participate.

Educational researchers and policymakers note analogies with the compulsory high school movement of the late 1800s and early 1900s; as economies evolve and employers require workers with new skills, large-scale change in the educational system may be necessary. Just as a shift to an industrial economy around the turn of the twentieth century necessitated high school education for all, so might the technological changes of the twenty-first century require a free system of pre-K through grade 14 education.

If community college does in fact become tuition-free, what are the implications for Promise programs? Existing two-year Promise programs would become redundant, but stakeholders in these communities could shift their attention to funding four-year options for eligible students, providing support for college costs beyond tuition, or investing in college access and preparedness initiatives. (Such transitions have already been required in some Tennessee communities.) The more expansive programs that currently provide support for a four-year option would not be greatly affected; even now, the relatively low cost of community college means that most of the dollars spent by the more expansive Promise programs flow to four-year institutions.

Another scenario, although an unlikely one, is that Pell Grant levels could be increased to cover a higher proportion of college costs. Pell Grants have steadily lost value over the past three decades; there has been some progress in increasing their value in recent years, but there is a lot of ground to make up. In 1979–1980, Pell Grants covered 99 percent of the total cost of attending a two-year institution and 77 percent of a four-year public institution; today, the respective numbers are 52 percent for two-year and 30 percent for four-year institutions (The Institute for College Access and Success 2014). Increases in Pell funding levels could make it less expensive for last-dollar Promise programs in high-poverty communities to operate, but the pace of college cost increases makes it inconceivable that Pell Grants will ever return to historic levels of coverage. And rising Pell Grants do nothing for middle-class students whose family incomes fall above the Pell cutoff and who are vulnerable to high levels of student debt. Even if additional resources do become available for low-income students, Promise programs will remain invaluable to middle-class families who are not eligible for need-based aid.

More probable policy developments include FAFSA simplification efforts, already well under way, which, when coupled with college access outreach initiatives, may result in higher uptake rates for available financial aid. (It is worth noting here that Promise programs do not appear to replace government financial aid as some observers fear. Many programs require FAFSA completion as a precondition to receiving the scholarship, and even in Kalamazoo, where that is not the case, FAFSA completion rates are actually higher than in surrounding districts.) In addition, state efforts to control tuition costs are likely to continue. These initiatives may make college slightly more affordable; however, despite rapid changes in the student financial aid landscape, there will continue to be an important role for place-based scholarships in substantially reducing tuition costs for a broad segment of local youth.

LEVERAGING PROMISE SCHOLARSHIPS FOR COMMUNITY CHANGE

A second set of questions concerns the track record of Promise programs, especially when it comes to transforming school districts and communities. What sets place-based scholarship programs apart from traditional financial aid approaches is that they are not simply a strategy to get more students to college. These programs seek to transform the culture of a school district by making an early promise of a scholarship to a high percentage of students at the beginning of their K–12 education. In this way, Promise programs can be expected to promote family engagement, student aspirations, and higher attainment, as well as district reforms that raise expectations, rigor, and relevance. Even more ambitious is the goal of transforming the broader community, more firmly attaching the people already living there and making it more attractive to new entrants who value education.

In earlier research, I have argued that the path through which Promise programs achieve these systemwide goals is indirect. The provision of funding alone does not change systems, but a well-designed scholarship program can serve as a catalyst for action on the part of many actors within the community. If these actors are aligned in their goals and coordinated in their strategies, then transformative change can be accomplished. Formally, this approach is known as collective impact and, as mentioned in Chapter 2, an entire industry has grown up around training community leaders in how to carry out collective impact strategies. While some of the tools and frameworks promoted by this industry can be helpful to communities' efforts to organize themselves, there is the danger of a one-size-fits-all approach that fails to fully take the local context into account.

We have learned during the 10 years since the Kalamazoo Promise was announced that a place-based scholarship can serve as a powerful catalyst for alignment. Moreover, the nature of this alignment will differ from community to community based on the mix of local assets and needs. But some Promise programs provide a bigger boost than others toward these transformative strategies. The following are characteristics and goals of Promise programs that best support community alignment.

Clarity around critical need. Program designers should be clear about the critical need they are trying to address with a Promise scholarship. As discussed in Chapter 4, design decisions have sometimes been driven by cost considerations rather than fit with critical need. If stakeholders are in agreement about an overarching critical need, then every element of program structure should flow from that. If a program is truly a response to a pressing local priority, then the financial resources and community buy-in necessary for its success will be easier to obtain. Kalamazoo's program has met with strong community support because its goal of strengthening the high-poverty school district that lies at the region's core resonates with individuals throughout the community. The Pittsburgh program has multiple goals that can be difficult to balance, in that it seeks to increase academic achievement, assist disadvantaged students, and promote economic revitalization. In another community that has long struggled with raising funds to complement its substantial college access efforts, a recently announced scholarship will be available (for now) only to the highest achieving (3.5 GPA) students who will be allowed to use it to attend one of two local colleges. Such students would generally choose to attend more selective institutions, and it is not clear what critical need is being met by creating incentives for students to undermatch. In short, the structure and rules of a Promise scholarship program should be devised with the community's critical need in mind. Only then will the incentives created by the program help accomplish the priorities of the community, making the job of alignment easier.

The perils of overpromising. A common pitfall in Promise communities is a tendency to oversell the expected impacts of a program in order to gain needed financial and public support. The old adage of "underpromise and overdeliver" holds great value for Promise communities that are engaged in what is essentially a long-term, large-scale experiment in social change. While most everyone involved in the Promise movement believes that place-based scholarships are a good idea, there is little hard evidence about what to expect from their implementation. Keeping expectations modest while understanding that many of the gains from Promise programs will emerge over decades are both essential messages for maintaining stakeholder support. The expectation of quick results that fail to materialize can rapidly dissipate the enthusiasm of funders and the public. Fine-tuning programs and engaging in continuous improvement based on data and results are essential practices as Promise programs seek to maximize their impact; however, when results are not immediate, the response may include cutbacks, retrenchment, or wholesale restructuring that bring about a whole new cycle of expectations. Of course, to students, families, and community members, the most important promise to keep is the scholarship itself; changes in scholarship terms or levels, or the complete elimination of a scholarship program, can do lasting damage to the Promise idea.

Keep it simple. One of the assets of the Kalamazoo Promise and several other Promise programs is their simplicity. To be able to summarize the program's terms in a sentence or two—go to school here, graduate from high school, and your college tuition will be paid—not only makes program administration easier and cheaper, it also helps with messaging and community buy-in. It is not essential to have generous donors in order to keep program structure simple. In Detroit, the message is similarly streamlined: attend and graduate from Detroit Public Schools, and you can attend one of five community colleges in the region tuition free. A Promise program will lead to community change only if it is widely used. Every condition or criterion added to the terms of a scholarship reduces the number of students who can use it and, hence, reduces its potential impact as a transformative tool.

One long-standing Promise program that has struggled with funding and concerns about student performance in college recently converted its terms to a tuition reimbursement program at the local community college, with the level of reimbursement dependent on high school attendance, GPA, ACT scores, extracurricular activities, and the writing of a thank-you note to the donors using the proper format. This program may succeed in saving the Promise organization some money and reducing the fund development task; however, it is also likely to reduce both impact and participation rates.

Early-commitment programs, such as the Legacy Scholars or Challenge Scholars, run a special risk here. These programs generally require students and families to sign up for the Promise at the end of elementary or beginning of middle school. Students must then meet a variety of behavioral, academic, and continual residency requirements over the next six years in order to receive a scholarship. While this approach can be useful in promoting higher achievement, parent engagement, and changes in school culture, after those six years, very few students are still likely to be eligible for the scholarship. (This is especially true in high-poverty districts, where family mobility is high.) While the complex requirements inherent in early-commitment programs are generally created with the best of intentions, they are ill suited to leveraging the kind of community alignment discussed above.

Attend to alignment. It would be a mistake to expect alignment to materialize automatically with the introduction of scholarship resources. Communication, coordination, cooperation, and collaboration must be pursued intentionally, whether formally or informally. There are many ways to structure such a process. In some communities, an official stakeholder group may exist; in Pittsburgh, for example, the board of the Pittsburgh Promise fills this role, while the Michigan Promise Zones are required by law to convene a Promise Zone Authority in each community. Ideally, such leadership groups are inclusive, broadly representative of the community, transparent in their operations, and open to grassroots input. In other communities, Promise programs have affiliated with other existing organizations, such as collective impact initiatives or college access networks. Kalamazoo, for all its advantages from a funding perspective, has done neither of these things. Instead, alignment has consisted mainly of efforts by individual organizations to adapt their work in support of Promise goals. The Kalamazoo Promise did serve as a catalyst for the creation of a countrywide collective action effort that ultimately led to the establishment of the Learning Network of Greater Kalamazoo, but for a variety of reasons this effort has failed to gain traction in the community as a whole. The tenth anniversary of the Kalamazoo Promise offers an opportunity to take stock of both the accomplishments and challenges that remain in using this generous pool of funds for deeper community change. Attention to alignment is a critical part of this conversation.

Can Promise programs succeed in the absence of effective community alignment? It depends on what is meant by success. At a minimum, Promise programs bring attention and resources to the college access movement, and there is evidence from multiple communities that place-based scholarships are increasing the percentage of students who attend college. There is also evidence that Promise programs are both stimulating and supporting K–12 school reforms that seek to prepare every child for some kind of postsecondary education or training. These are substantial successes. But the place-based scholarship concept promises more, and this deeper success requires alignment. If students who are struggling academically or behaviorally in the K–12 setting are to make use of a scholarship, they will need tutoring, counseling, mentoring, and out-of-school time resources often provided by community-based organizations. If these students are to succeed once in college, they will need support services at the postsecondary level. If cities are to attract and retain population as a result of a Promise program, there will need to be buy-in from municipal officials, realtors, businesses, and economic development leaders. In short, to leverage a place-based scholarship for transformative change, whether of a school district or the city in which it is located, alignment is essential.

Invest in research and evaluation. It is also essential that Promise programs have a research and evaluation component. Simply put, without it they will be unable to demonstrate their impact either to local stakeholders or a broader national audience. Thus far, federally funded research efforts have been disappointing. The Department of Education has awarded only a handful grants to study Promise programs, the first to a group of researchers at Western Michigan University (WMU) in Kalamazoo to survey students, teachers, and parents about how the Kalamazoo Promise affected their attitudes and aspirations. Unfortunately, this research was not tied to concrete measures of achievement, so it is impossible to know if a student who says he is going to work harder and get better grades does indeed do that. A second grant was for a study of The Degree Project, the Milwaukee Public Schools program that used a randomized controlled assignment method to determine which schools would receive the Promise program. The study, however, will tell us little about the broader impact of Promise programs because only one cohort of ninth graders in each selected school was eligible to receive the scholarship; thus, the peer and school culture effects one sees in Promise communities, and that are undoubtedly important elements in achievement gains, were missing. The third grant, awarded in 2015 by the Department of Education through its "First in the World" program, will allow researchers at WMU to test a range of strategies, including mentorship, to increase degree completion by Promise students. While the findings of this project are designed to be relevant beyond Kalamazoo, it will be interesting to see whether this research effort also contributes to the alignment challenge mentioned above—that is, to what degree will WMU's efforts to test mentoring strategies be connected to other community-based efforts to ensure college success for Promise-eligible students?

The federal government's preference for randomized controlled trials, and the virtual impossibility of examining a districtwide Promise program through that lens, means that evaluation resources probably need to come from other sources. Some Promise programs, with Pittsburgh in the lead, have invested heavily in research and evaluation, commissioning multiple studies from the RAND Corporation, McKinsey & Company, and the University of Pittsburgh, the findings of which are used to inform program changes in the kind of continuous improvement process that is central to collective impact. Other evaluation efforts have relied on local resources; for example, almost all the existing research into the Kalamazoo Promise has been carried out with resources of the Upjohn Institute in Kalamazoo (publisher of this book), with some support from outside foundations.

One of the more exciting developments on the research horizon is the linking of scholars across multiple communities into a Promise Research Consortium, led by the Upjohn Institute and funded initially by the Lumina Foundation. This is the first effort to generate comparative research into Promise programs; ideally, future research efforts will link to and build upon this foundation. As part of the effort, a set of materials is being developed to support new Promise programs in understanding which indicators to track as part of their evaluation effort, when, and why. The networking among researchers that has been under way for several years is beginning to pay off with the creation of this new body of research.

CONCLUDING THOUGHTS

The Promise idea has emanated from many different sources. In Kalamazoo, the idea was pioneered by a group of wealthy residents seeking to make a transformative investment in their community. In El Dorado, the CEO of the town's largest employer took the lead with hopes of reversing negative economic trends. In Pittsburgh, the district superintendent, mayor, and leading employer teamed up to reinforce reform efforts under way in the schools and build on improvements under way in the local economy. Denver's wealthy donors were seeking, above all, to pave the way for more low-income students to attend college. In my time studying Promise programs, I have spoken with school board members, businesspeople, economic development officials, foundation officers, and concerned citizens, all attracted by the powerful idea of investing in education to ensure the vitality of their community. While a Promise program can indeed be launched by a small group of committed individuals, engagement with the broader community is essential if community transformation is to be accomplished.

The Promise movement is characterized by an inherent tension between local efforts and the benefits that can come from sharing information and resources across communities. Thus far, the balance has been very much in a local direction. The hallmark of the Promise movement is local innovation in response to local needs. In fact, one can question whether this diverse collection of initiatives should be thought of as a movement at all. But the linkages among Promise stakeholders have proven robust and advantageous, and not just to the researchers mentioned above. Leaders in Promise communities have sought each other out and through informal interaction and the formal opportunities provided by almost-annual PromiseNet conferences engaged in a deep and authentic process of mutual learning. Maintaining this balance between local impetus and program heterogeneity, while promoting best practices and continuous improvement, is a central challenge for the future.

In the decade since the Kalamazoo Promise was announced, we have witnessed grassroots innovation meeting the human capital needs of individuals and communities. The next 10 years will, ideally, draw on the lessons learned from this initial period—how to structure a Promise program to meet critical needs and achieve maximum impact; how to ensure that all students in a community can take advantage of the opportunities available to them, making Promise programs an engine for reducing inequality; and how to create effective alignment around the ambitious task of community change. As the process of innovation continues, I hope that stakeholders will learn from the lessons presented in this book, making decisions grounded in evidence to advance the goals of their Promise programs. By doing so, they will continue to offer inspiration to others seeking to make their communities better places to live.

Appendix A
List of Promise Programs

Program name	Location	Announced	Type	Requirements	Award	Eligible schools
Arkadelphia Promise	Arkadelphia, AR	2010	Targeted, expansive	• Graduate from Arkadelphia Public Schools • Continuous enrollment since 9th grade • 2.5 GPA and/or 19 ACT • Receive AR Academic Challenge (Lottery) Scholarship • Apply for 2 "outside" scholarships	Sliding scale; 65–100% of unmet need; Maximum: resident tuition at AR public university	Any accredited postsecondary institution (PSI) in the U.S.
Baldwin Promise[a]	Baldwin, MI	2009	Universal, expansive	• Live within Baldwin Public School District Boundaries since 9th grade	Sliding scale; up to $5,000 per year	Any accredited PSI in Michigan
Battle Creek Promise[a]	Battle Creek, MI	2009	Targeted, restrictive	• Graduate from high school while paying taxes into the Battle Creek Public School District • Continuous enrollment since 9th grade • Articulates with Legacy Scholars	100% of unmet need for tuition and fees	Kellogg Community College

Program	Location	Year	Type	Eligibility	Award	Eligible Institutions
Bay Commitment	Bay City, MI	2007	Targeted, restrictive	• Graduate from Bay County high schools • Continuous enrollment since 9th grade • Continuous residency since 7th grade • First-generation college-going student	$2,000	Delta College; Saginaw Valley State University
Beacon of Hope[b]	Lynchburg, VA	2011	TBD	• Graduate from Lynchburg City Schools • Continuous enrollment since 9th grade	Future Centers established; scholarship not yet launched	TBD
Benton Harbor Promise[a]	Benton Harbor, MI	2011	Universal, expansive	• Graduate from any high school within Benton Harbor school district boundaries • Continuous enrollment since 9th grade	Full tuition and fees for any community college; $4,400 per year for 2 years at 4-year institutions	Any accredited PSI in Michigan
Challenge Scholars[b]	Grand Rapids, MI	2013	Targeted, expansive	• Graduate from Union High School • Continuous enrollment since 6th grade • 2.0 GPA • Attendance and behavior	Up to 100% of unmet need depending on financial need	Any accredited public PSI in Michigan and 2 accredited private PSIs

Program name	Location	Announced	Type	Requirements	Award	Eligible schools
Chicago Star Scholarship	Chicago, IL	2014	Targeted, restrictive	• Graduate from Chicago Public Schools • 3.0 GPA	100% of unmet need	Chicago City Schools
Cleveland County Promise	Cleveland, NC	2012	Universal, expansive	• Graduate from Cleveland County High School • 85% attendance • Completion of online financial literacy course	Sliding scale; 50–100% unmet need; Maximum: resident tuition at NC public university	Any accredited PSI in U.S.
College Bound	Hammond, IN	2006	Targeted, expansive	• Graduate from Hammond high schools • Demonstrate residence in owner-occupied home • 3.0 GPA, 21 ACT and/ or 1000–1400 SAT	Sliding scale; up to $10,500 per year	Any accredited PSI in U.S.
CORE Promise Scholarship	Philadelphia, PA	2003	Universal, expansive	• Graduate from Philadelphia-area high school • Resident of City of Philadelphia	$250	21 public PSIs in Pennsylvania

Program	Location	Year	Type	Eligibility	Award	Institutions
Denver Scholarship Foundation	Denver, CO	2006	Targeted, expansive	• Graduate from Denver Public Schools • Continuous enrollment since 9th grade • 2.0 GPA • Demonstrate financial need	Sliding scale; $1,100–$3,400 per year depending on financial need and PSI	32 PSIs in Colorado
Detroit Scholarship Fund[a]	Detroit, MI	2013	Universal, restrictive	• Graduate from any high school in the city of Detroit • Continuous enrollment since 10th grade	100% of unmet need	5 Detroit-area community colleges
Dyer County Promise	Dyer County, TN	2006	Universal, restrictive	• Graduate from Dyer County high schools • Continuous enrollment since 9th grade	Sliding scale; up to $675 per year (4 semesters)	Dyersburg State Community College; Tennessee Technology Center
Educate and Grow[b]	Carter, Johnson, Sullivan, Washington, and Unicoi Counties, TN	2001	Universal, restrictive	• Graduate from participating county high school • Continuous enrollment since 11th grade		Northeastern State University

Program name	Location	Announced	Type	Requirements	Award	Eligible schools
El Dorado Promise	El Dorado, AR	2007	Universal, expansive	• Graduate from El Dorado Public School District • Continuous enrollment since 9th grade	Sliding scale; 65%–100% of tuition; Maximum: resident tuition at AR public university	Any accredited PSI in the U.S.
Galesburg Promise	Galesburg, IL	2014	Universal, restrictive	• Graduate from Galesburg High School • Continuous enrollment since 10th grade	Sliding scale; 50%–100% of unmet need; prorated on enrollment (4 semesters)	Carl Sandburg College
Garrett County Scholarship Program	Garrett County, MD	2006	Universal, restrictive	• Graduate from Garrett County Public Schools • Continuous enrollment since 10th grade	Full tuition (4 semesters)	Garrett College
Great River Promise	Mississippi County, AR	2009	Universal, restrictive	• Graduate from Mississippi County • Continuous enrollment since 9th grade • 95% attendance	Full tuition (4 semesters)	Arkansas Northeastern College

Program	Location	Year	Type	Eligibility	Award amount	PSI eligibility
Harper College Promise[b]	Palatine, IL	2015	Targeted, restrictive	• Graduate from Districts 211, 214, or 220 • 2.0–3.2 GPA • Attendance and community service	Full tuition (4 semesters)	Harper College
Hartford Promise[b]	Hartford, CT	2013	Targeted, expansive	• Graduate from Hartford Public Schools • Continuous enrollment since 9th grade • 3.0 GPA	Sliding scale; $2,500–$5,000 depending on PSI	Any accredited PSI in the U.S.
Hazel Park Promise[a]	Hazel Park, MI	2011	Universal, expansive	• Graduate from Hazel Park High School • Live within school district	Sliding scale; up to amount of 62 credits at Oakland Community College or $2,000 for 2 years elsewhere (4 semesters)	Any accredited PSI in Michigan
Holland-Zeeland Promise	Holland, MI	2010	Targeted, expansive	• Graduate from Holland-Zeeland high schools • Demonstrate financial need	$2,500–$15,000 depending on financial need	Any accredited PSI in Michigan

Program name	Location	Announced	Type	Requirements	Award	Eligible schools
H.O.P.E. Scholarship	Lansing, MI	2001	Targeted, restrictive	• Graduate from High School in the Lansing Public School District • Continuous enrollment since 6th grade • Attend H.O.P.E. Scholarship events	Full tuition and fees, with assistance for books	Lansing Community College
Hopkinsville Rotary Scholars	Hopkinsville, KY	2007	Targeted, restrictive	• Graduate from Christian County high schools • 2.5 GPA • 95% attendance	100% of unmet need (4 semesters)	Hopkinsville Community College
Jackson Legacy	Jackson, MI	2006	Targeted, restrictive	• Graduate from Jackson County high schools • 2.5 GPA • Community service	$1,000 one time	Jackson College; Spring Arbor University; Baker College of Jackson
Kalamazoo Promise	Kalamazoo, MI	2005	Universal, expansive	• Graduate from Kalamazoo Public Schools • Continuous enrollment since 9th grade	Sliding scale; 65%–100% of tuition depending on length of enrollment	Any accredited public PSI in Michigan; for class of 2015 on, 15 private colleges included

Program	Location	Year	Type	Eligibility Requirements	Award	Participating Institutions
La Crosse Promise[b]	La Crosse, WI	2012	Targeted; expansive	• Graduate from La Crosse School District • Home ownership or rehabilitation in city of La Crosse	Future Centers established; scholarship not yet launched	Any accredited PSI in Wisconsin
Lansing Promise[a]	Lansing, MI	2009	Universal, restrictive	• Graduate from any high school within Lansing School District boundaries	Up to 65 credits at LCC or equivalent applied to Michigan State University (approximately $5,800)	Lansing Community College; Michigan State University
Legacy Scholars	Battle Creek, MI	2005	Universal, restrictive	• Graduate from Lakeview or Battle Creek Public Schools	Sliding scale; 50%–100% of unmet need depending on length of enrollment	Kellogg Community College
Long Beach College Promise	Long Beach, CA	2008	Universal, restrictive	• Graduate from Long Beach Unified School District • Additional requirements apply for admission to California State University, Long Beach	Full tuition to LBCC (1 semester); Guaranteed admission to CSU, Long Beach	Long Beach City College; California State University, Long Beach

Program name	Location	Announced	Type	Requirements	Award	Eligible schools
Montgomery County Ohio College Promise	Dayton, OH	2011	Targeted, restrictive	• Graduate from Dayton-area high school • Continuous enrollment since 8th grade • Demonstrate financial need and academic achievement • Pledge to maintain good behavior and citizenship	Full tuition (4–6 semesters) depending on PSI	Sinclair Community College; 7 4-year PSIs in Ohio
New Haven Promise	New Haven, CT	2010	Targeted, expansive	• Graduate from New Haven Public Schools • Continuous enrollment since 9th grade • 3.0 GPA • 90% attendance • Community service	Sliding scale; 65%–100% of unmet need, up to $10,000 per year	Any accredited public PSI in Connecticut
Northport Promise	Northport, MI	2007	Targeted, expansive	• Graduate from Northport High School • Continuous enrollment since 9th grade • 2.0 GPA • Participation in fund-raising activities	Sliding scale; 50%–100% of unmet need depending on length of enrollment and fund-raising participation	Any accredited PSI in Michigan

Program	Location	Year	Type	Requirements	Award	College Partners
Partners Advancing College Education (PACE) Promise	San Marcos, CA	2007	Targeted, restrictive	• Graduate from San Marcos Unified School District • Continuous enrollment since 9th grade • 2.0 GPA • Complete college preparatory coursework	Guaranteed admission; $1,000 for up to 4 years	California State University of San Marcos
Pensacola Pledge Scholars	Pensacola, FL	2012	Universal, restrictive	• Graduate from Escambia High School • Live in Pensacola city limits	$1,200 –$2,000 per year depending on PSI	Pensacola State College; University of West Florida
Peoria Promise	Peoria, IL	2006	Targeted, restrictive	• Graduate from Peoria high schools • Continuous enrollment since 10th grade • Benefit percentage calculated by point system based on various factors	Sliding scale; 25%–100% tuition reimbursement (64 credit hours)	Illinois Central College

Program name	Location	Announced	Type	Requirements	Award	Eligible schools
Pittsburgh Promise	Pittsburgh, PA	2006	Targeted, expansive	• Graduate from Pittsburgh Public Schools • Continuous enrollment since 9th grade • 2.5 GPA • 90% attendance	Sliding scale; $7,500 per year depending on length of enrollment	Any accredited PSI in Pennsylvania
Pontiac Promise[a]	Pontiac, MI	2009	Universal, expansive	• Graduate from any high school within the Pontiac School District boundaries • Continuous enrollment from 6th grade	Up to 65 credits at Oakland Community College or 3 years (whichever comes first)	Any accredited PSI in Michigan
Promise for the Future	Pinal County, AZ	2006	Targeted, restrictive	• Graduate from Pinal County high schools • Continuous enrollment since 8th grade • Sign contract of commitment in 8th grade • 2.75 GPA • Community service	Full tuition (4 semesters)	Central Arizona College

Program	Location	Year	Type	Eligibility	Award	PSI
Rochester Promise	Rochester, NY	2007	Targeted, restrictive	• Graduate from Rochester City School District • Continuous enrollment since 11th grade • Demonstrate financial need	100% of unmet need; up to $25,000 per year (8 semesters)	University of Rochester
Rockford Promise	Rockford, IL	2008	Universal, expansive	• Graduate from Rockford Public School District • Complete FAFSA	$1,000 awards to students drawn at random	Any accredited PSI in the U.S.
Rusk TJC Citizens Promise	Tyler, TX	2014	Targeted, restrictive	• Graduate from Rusk High School • 2.5 GPA • Perform in top 1/2 of graduating class	Up to $8,000 per year (4 semesters)	Tyler Junior College
Saginaw Promise[a]	Saginaw, MI	2012	Universal, expansive	• Graduate from a Saginaw Public Schools high school • Live within school district boundaries • Continuous enrollment since 9th grade	Sliding scale; Last-dollar coverage of tuition and fees for 2-year programs; $2,000 per year for 2 years for 4-year programs	Any accredited PSI in Michigan

Program name	Location	Announced	Type	Requirements	Award	Eligible schools
Say Yes to Education, Buffalo	Buffalo, NY	2011	Universal, expansive	• Graduate from Buffalo Public Schools • Continuous enrollment since 9th grade	Sliding scale; 65%–100% of unmet need	Any PSI in City University of New York (CUNY) or State University of New York (SUNY) system, as well as private college partners with a $75,000 income cap
Say Yes to Education, Syracuse	Syracuse, NY	2009	Universal, expansive	• Graduate from Syracuse City School District • Continuous enrollment since 10th grade	100% of unmet need	Any college in CUNY or SUNY system as well as private partners with same income cap as Say Yes, Buffalo
School Counts!	Madisonville, KY	2010	Targeted, restrictive	• Graduate from Hopkins County Schools • Continuous enrollment since 9th grade • 2.5 GPA • 95% attendance	$2,000 per year (4 semesters)	Madisonville Community College
Tangelo Park Program	Tangelo Park, FL	1993	Universal; expansive	• Graduate from Dr. Phillips high school • Continuous enrollment since 11th grade	Full tuition, room, board and living expenses (8 semesters)	Any accredited PSI in Florida

	Location	Year	Type	Eligibility	Award	College
tnAchieves	Knoxville, TN	2008	Universal, expansive	• Graduate from Tennessee high school	Sliding scale; up to $4,000 per year (5 semesters)	Any accredited technical or community college in Tennessee
Tulsa Achieves	Tulsa, OK	2007	Targeted, restrictive	• Graduate from Tulsa Area schools • 2.0 GPA	Sliding scale; 25%–100% of tuition depending on length of enrollment	Tulsa Community College
Ventura College Promise	Ventura County, CA	2006	Universal, restrictive	• Graduate from Ventura County high schools	Full tuition (2 semesters)	Ventura College

[a] Michigan Promise Zone.
[b] Not currently granting scholarships.

NOTE: This list contains Promise programs active as of August 2015. It represents a best effort by Upjohn Institute staff to include programs that meet our definition. We recognize that other, similar place-based scholarships may exist and that new programs continue to be launched. An updated list of Promise programs and map reside on the Upjohn Institute website, www.upjohn.org. Please consult it for the newest information, and contact the Institute if you believe you should be added to the database.

References

Andrews, Rodney J. 2013. "The Promise of 'Promise' Programs." Paper prepared for the American Enterprise Institute conference, "The Trillion-Dollar Question: Reinventing Student Financial Aid for the 21st Century," held in Washington, DC, June 24.

Ash, Jennifer W., and Gary W. Ritter. 2014. "Early Impacts of the El Dorado Promise on Enrollment and Achievement." *Arkansas Education Report* 11(1). Fayetteville, AR: University of Arkansas Office of Education Policy. http://www.officeforeducationpolicy.org/wp-content/uploads/El-Dorado-Promise-AER.pdf (accessed August 7, 2015).

Bartik, Timothy J., Randall Eberts, and Wei-Jang Huang. 2010. "The Kalamazoo Promise, and Enrollment and Achievement Trends in Kalamazoo Public Schools." Working paper presented at the PromiseNet 2010 Conference, held in Kalamazoo, MI, June 16–18.

Bartik, Timothy J., Brad J. Hershbein, and Marta Lachowska. 2015. "The Effects of the Kalamazoo Promise Scholarship on College Enrollment, Persistence, and Completion." Upjohn Institute Working Paper No. 15-229. Kalamazoo, MI: W.E. Upjohn Institute for Employment Research.

Bartik, Timothy J., and Marta Lachowska. 2012. "The Short-Term Effects of the Kalamazoo Promise Scholarship on Student Outcomes." Upjohn Institute Working Paper No. 12-186. Kalamazoo, MI: W.E. Upjohn Institute for Employment Research.

Bernholz, Lucy. 2011. "Philanthropy Buzzwords of 2011." *Chronicle of Philanthropy*, December 27. https://philanthropy.com/article/Philanthropy-Buzzwords-of-2011/157395 (accessed August 7, 2015).

Bettinger, Eric P., Bridget Terry Long, and Philip Oreopoulous. 2013. "The FAFSA Project: Results from the H&R Block FAFSA Experiment and Next Steps." Cambridge, MA: Harvard University.

Chourey, Sarita. 2006. "Buzz Big after ABC Promise Report." *Kalamazoo Gazette*, September 9, A:1.

Chute, Eleanor. 2014. "Pittsburgh Promise Loosens Scholarship Restrictions for Technical Programs." *Pittsburgh Post-Gazette*, June 18. http://www.post-gazette.com/news/education/2014/06/19/Pittsburgh-Promise-loosens-scholarship-restrictions-for-technical-programs/stories/201406190071 (accessed August 7, 2015).

———. 2015. "Effort Aims to Help Black Male Students Qualify for Pittsburgh Promise." *Pittsburgh Post-Gazette*, January 30. http://www.post-gazette.com/news/education/2015/01/30/Effort-aims-to-help-black-male-students-qualify-for-Pittsburgh-Promise/stories/201501290160 (accessed August 13, 2015).

College Bound. 2013. *2013 Scholarship Status Report.* Denver: College Bound Scholarship Program.

―――. 2014. *Trends in College Pricing, 2014.* New York: College Board.

Cornwell, Christopher M., David B. Mustard, and Deepa Sridhar. 2006. "The Enrollment Effects of Merit-Based Financial Aid: Evidence from Georgia's HOPE Scholarship." *Journal of Labor Economics* 24(4): 761–786.

Denver Public Schools. 2014. *High School Outcomes Analysis: Report to the Board of Education, 2012–13 School Year Results.* Denver: Denver Public Schools.

Dreier, Peter, John Mollenkopf, and Todd Swanstrom. 2001. *Place Matters: Metropolitics for the Twenty-First Century.* Lawrence, KS: University Press of Kansas.

Dynarski, Susan. 2000. "Hope for Whom? Financial Aid for the Middle Class and Its Impact on College Attendance." NBER Working Paper No. 7756. Cambridge, MA: National Bureau for Economic Research.

―――. 2004. "The New Merit Aid." In *College Choices: The Economics of Where to Go, When to Go, and How to Pay For It,* Caroline M. Hoxby, ed. Cambridge, MA: National Bureau for Economic Research, pp. 63–100.

Dynarski, Susan M., and Judith E. Scott-Clayton. 2007. "College Grants on a Postcard: A Proposal for Simple and Predictable Federal Student Aid." Hamilton Project Discussion Paper No. 2007-01. Washington, DC: Brookings Institution.

El Dorado Promise. 2015. "El Dorado Promise Creates College-Going Culture in El Dorado Public Schools." January 22. www.eldoradopromise.com/news/ (accessed August 13, 2015).

FSG. N.d. "What Is Collective Impact?" http://www.fsg.org/approach-areas/collective-impact (accessed August 13, 2015).

Glaeser, Edward L. 2011. *Triumph of the City: How Our Greatest Invention Makes Us Richer, Smarter, Greener, Healthier, and Happier.* New York: Penguin Press.

Glaeser, Edward L., and Christopher R. Berry. 2006. "Why Are Smart Places Getting Smarter?" Rappaport Institute/Taubman Center Policy Brief, PB-2006-2. Cambridge, MA: Harvard University, John F. Kennedy School of Government.

Glaeser, Edward L., and Albert Saiz. 2003. "The Rise of the Skilled City." Harvard Institute of Economic Research Discussion Paper No. 2025. Cambridge, MA: Harvard University.

Gonzalez, Gabriella C., Robert Bozick, Shannah Tharp-Taylor, and Andrea Phillips. 2011. "Fulfilling the Pittsburgh Promise: Early Progress of Pittsburgh's Postsecondary Scholarship Program." Santa Monica: RAND Corporation.

Great Lakes Higher Education Corporation. 2015. "400 MPS Grads Eligible for $5 Million in College Scholarships from The Degree Project." News release, August 13. Madison, WI: Great Lakes Higher Education Guaranty Corporation. http://www.nasfaa.org/uploads/documents/great_lakes _commits_5million.pdf (accessed August 19, 2015).

Hamill, Sean D. 2008. "Inside the Promise." *Pittsburgh Quarterly*, Spring. http://www.pittsburghquarterly.com/index.php/Education/inside-the -promise.html (accessed August 7, 2015).

Harris, Douglas N. 2013. "Is Traditional Financial Aid Too Little, Too Late to Help Youth Succeed in College? An Introduction to the Degree Project Promise Scholarship Experiment." *New Directions for Youth Development* 140: 99–116. doi: 10.1002/yd.20080 (accessed August 7, 2015).

Heller, Donald E. 2006. "MCAS Scores and the Adams Scholarships: A Policy Failure." Policy Brief for the Civil Rights Project at Harvard University. University Park, PA: Center for the Study of Higher Education at Pennsylvania State University.

Hershbein, Brad J. 2013. "A Second Look at Enrollment Changes after the Kalamazoo Promise." Upjohn Institute Working Paper No. 13-200. Kalamazoo, MI: W.E. Upjohn Institute for Employment Research.

Hershbein, Brad, and Kevin M. Hollenbeck, eds. 2015. *Student Loans and the Dynamics of Debt*. Kalamazoo, MI: W.E. Upjohn Institute for Employment Research.

Hoxby, Caroline M., and Sarah Turner. 2013. "Informing Students about Their College Options: A Proposal for Broadening the Expanding College Opportunities Project." Hamilton Project Discussion Paper No. 2013-03. Washington, DC: Brookings Institution.

Iriti, Jennifer, William Bickel, and Julie Kaufman. 2012. "Realizing 'The Promise': Scholar Retention and Persistence in Post-Secondary Education." Pittsburgh, PA: University of Pittsburgh, Learning Research and Development Center.

Jessup, Kathy. 2005. "Kalamazoo Rated among 100 Best Places for Kids." *Kalamazoo Gazette*, January 25, A:1.

Kahlenberg, Richard D., ed. 2012. *The Future of School Integration: Socioeconomic Diversity as an Education Reform Strategy*. New York: Century Foundation.

Kania, John, and Mark Kramer. 2011. "Collective Impact." *Stanford Social Innovation Review* 9(1): 36–41.

Katz, Bruce. 2006. "Six Ways Cities Can Reach Their Economic Potential." *Diverse Perspectives on Critical Issues, Living Cities Policy Series*, Vol. 1. Washington, DC: Living Cities, the National Community Development Initiative.

LeGower, Michael, and Randall Walsh. 2014. "Promise Scholarship Programs as Place-Making Policy: Evidence from School Enrollment and Housing Prices." NBER Working Paper No. 20056. Cambridge, MA: National Bureau of Economic Research.

Lord, Rich. 2006. "Tuition Grants a Lure for City Schools." *Pittsburgh Post -Gazette*, December 14. http://www.post-gazette.com/local/city/2006/12/14/Tuition-grants-a-lure-for-city-schools/stories/200612140353 (accessed August 7, 2015).

Mack, Julie. 2014. "Kalamazoo Public Schools Catching Up to More Affluent Districts, Superintendent Says." *Kalamazoo Gazette*, October 27. http://www.mlive.com/news/kalamazoo/index.ssf/2014/10/kalamazoo_public _schools_catch.html (accessed July 7, 2015).

———. 2015a. "Kalamazoo Promise Donors: 'We Will Be With You for Generations to Come.'" Mlive.com, August 15. http://www.mlive.com/news/kalamazoo/index.ssf/2015/08/kalamazoo_promise_donors_offer .html (accessed August 19, 2015).

———. 2015b. "Kalamazoo Public Schools Graduation Rate Is Up, But Data Also Shows District's Challenges." Mlive.com, March 12. http://www.mlive.com/news/kalamazoo/index.ssf/2014/10/kalamazoo_public _schools_catch.html (accessed July 29, 2015).

McKinsey & Company. 2007. "The Pittsburgh Promise: Case Study of Promises in Kalamazoo and Other Communities." December 5. New York: McKinsey & Company.

Miller-Adams, Michelle. 2009a. *The Power of a Promise: Education and Economic Renewal in Kalamazoo*. Kalamazoo, MI: W.E. Upjohn Institute for Employment Research.

———. 2009b. "The Kalamazoo Promise and the Diffusion of a Private Policy Innovation." Paper presented at the Midwest Political Science Association annual conference, held in Chicago, April.

———. 2015. "The Evolution of the Promise Scholarship Movement: Replication, Reinvention, and Critical Design Choices." Paper presented at American Educational Research Association 2015 Annual Meeting, held in Chicago, April 16–20.

Miller-Adams, Michelle, and Jenna Fiore. 2013. "The Kalamazoo Promise and Changing Perceptions of the Kalamazoo Public Schools." Policy Paper No. 2013-016. Kalamazoo, MI: W.E. Upjohn Institute for Employment Research.

Miller-Adams, Michelle, and Bridget Timmeney. 2013. "The Impact of the Kalamazoo Promise on College Choice: An Analysis of Kalamazoo Area Math and Science Center Graduates." Policy Paper No. 2013-014. Kalamazoo, MI: W.E. Upjohn Institute for Employment Research.

Miron, Gary, Jeffrey N. Jones, and Allison J. Kelaher-Young. 2009. "The

Impact of the Kalamazoo Promise on Student Attitudes, Goals, and Aspirations." Working Paper No. 6. Kalamazoo, MI: Western Michigan University.

Pell Institute. 2015. "Investing in Denver's Workforce and Economic Future: The Benefits of the Denver Scholarship Foundation." Washington, DC; Littleton, CO: Pell Institute for the Study of Opportunity in Higher Education and Development Research Partners. http://www.denverscholarship .org/sites/default/files/multi_file/subsection/download/2015%20Econ %20Impact%20Study.pdf (accessed August 7, 2015).

"Pittsburgh Promise Adjusts Program to Benefit More Pittsburgh Students." 2015. News release. http://pittsburghpromise.org/assets/documents/news _7_14.pdf (accessed July 29, 2015).

Rogers, Everett M. 2003. *Diffusion of Innovations*, 5th ed. New York: Free Press.

Schleis, Paula. 2015. "LeBron James Announces Full Scholarships to University of Akron for His I PROMISE Kids." *Akron Beacon Journal*, August 13. http://www.ohio.com/news/break-news/lebron-james-announces-full -scholarships-to-university-of-akron-for-his-i-promise-kids-1.616033 (accessed August 19, 2015).

Schuch, Sarah. 2014. "Flint Promise: Local Legislators Hope to Bring More Scholarship Funds to Flint Students." Mlive.com, February 27. http://www .mlive.com/news/flint/index.ssf/2014/02/flint_promise_local_legislator .html (accessed August 13, 2015).

Scott-Clayton, Judith. 2011. "On Money and Motivation: A Quasi-Experimental Analysis of Financial Incentives for College Achievement." *Journal of Human Resources* 46(3): 614–646.

Shipan, Charles R., and Craig Volden. 2008. "The Mechanisms of Policy Diffusion." *American Journal of Political Science* 52(4): 840–857.

———. 2012. "Policy Diffusion: Seven Lessons for Scholars and Practitioners." *Public Administration Review* 72(6): 788–796.

Sjoquist, David L., and John V. Winters. 2014. "Merit Aid and Post-College Retention in the State." *Journal of Urban Economics* 80: 39–50.

Sugrue, Thomas J. 1996. *The Origins of the Urban Crisis: Race and Inequality in Postwar Detroit*, rev. ed. 2005. Princeton, NJ: Princeton University Press.

The Institute for College Access and Success. 2014. "Pell Grants Help Keep College Affordable for Millions of Americans." http://ticas.org/sites/ default/files/pub_files/Overall_Pell_one-pager.pdf (accessed August 7, 2015).

Thredgold, Jeff. 2007. "'Promise(d)' Land." *Tea Leaf.* Thredgold Economic Associates. January 17. www.thredgold.com (accessed September 15, 2015).

Times of Northwest Indiana. 2014. "Hammond College Bound Scholarship Program Benefits Local Families." July 9. http://www.nwitimes .com/news/local/lake/hammond/hammond-college-bound-scholarship -program-benefits-local-families/article_f50dd3d1-19a0-590b-a59e -6f8bb1bc9520.html (accessed August 7, 2015).

U.S. Department of Education. National Center for Education Statistics. 2014. *The Condition of Education 2014.* NCES 2014-083. Washington, DC: U.S. Department of Education.

Vaade, Elizabeth, and Bo McCready. 2011. "Which Students to Serve? Universal or Targeted Eligibility for Postsecondary Opportunity Programs." Policy brief. Madison, WI: Wisconsin Center for the Advancement of Postsecondary Education.

Wiggins, Rosalind Z. 2014. *PromiseNet: Toward a More Unified Network?* New Haven, CT: Yale School of Management Case Study.

White House. 2015. "White House Unveils America's College Promise Proposal: Tuition-Free Community College for Responsible Students." White House Fact Sheet, January 9. Washington, DC: White House.

Author

Dr. Michelle Miller-Adams is the author of three previous books and an expert on community-building and economic development. She received her PhD in political science and her master's degree in international affairs from Columbia University, and her bachelor's degree in history from the University of California, Santa Barbara, graduating Phi Beta Kappa. Her professional career has spanned the fields of nonprofit management, finance, research, and academia; positions have included consultant to the W.K. Kellogg Foundation, vice president for programs at the Twentieth Century Fund (now the Century Foundation), and vice president for research at a Wall Street investment bank.

Miller-Adams was the principal investigator for a Ford Foundation–sponsored research project concerning asset-based strategies for fighting poverty, a project that resulted in the publication of *Owning Up: Poverty, Assets, and the American Dream* (Brookings Institution Press, 2002). She is currently a research fellow at the W.E. Upjohn Institute for Employment Research, where she wrote *The Power of a Promise: Education and Economic Renewal in Kalamazoo* (W.E. Upjohn Institute, 2009), and an associate professor of political science at Grand Valley State University.

Index

The italic letters *f*, *n*, or *t* following a page number indicate a figure, note, or table on that page. Double letters mean more than one such item on a single page.

129

About the Institute

The W.E. Upjohn Institute for Employment Research is a nonprofit research organization devoted to finding and promoting solutions to employment-related problems at the national, state, and local levels. It is an activity of the W.E. Upjohn Unemployment Trustee Corporation, which was established in 1932 to administer a fund set aside by Dr. W.E. Upjohn, founder of The Upjohn Company, to seek ways to counteract the loss of employment income during economic downturns.

The Institute is funded largely by income from the W.E. Upjohn Unemployment Trust, supplemented by outside grants, contracts, and sales of publications. Activities of the Institute comprise the following elements: 1) a research program conducted by a resident staff of professional social scientists; 2) a competitive grant program, which expands and complements the internal research program by providing financial support to researchers outside the Institute; 3) a publications program, which provides the major vehicle for disseminating the research of staff and grantees, as well as other selected works in the field; and 4) an Employment Management Services division, which manages most of the publicly funded employment and training programs in the local area.

The broad objectives of the Institute's research, grant, and publication programs are to 1) promote scholarship and experimentation on issues of public and private employment and unemployment policy, and 2) make knowledge and scholarship relevant and useful to policymakers in their pursuit of solutions to employment and unemployment problems.

Current areas of concentration for these programs include causes, consequences, and measures to alleviate unemployment; social insurance and income maintenance programs; compensation; workforce quality; work arrangements; family labor issues; labor-management relations; the Kalamazoo Promise and other place-based scholarship programs; and regional economic development and local labor markets.

CPSIA information can be obtained
at www.ICGtesting.com
Printed in the USA
FFOW04n1725221015